80 POEMS OR SO

IVOR GURNEY

---

80 POEMS OR SO

EDITED BY

GEORGE WALTER

&

R.K.R. THORNTON

Mid Northumberland Arts Group

Carcanet Press

1997

First published in 1997 by
Mid Northumberland Arts Group
Wansbeck Square
Ashington
Northumberland NE63 9XL

in association with

Carcanet Press Limited
4th Floor, Conavon Court
12–16 Blackfriars Street
Manchester M3 5BQ

A CIP catalogue record for this book
is available from the British Library
ISBN 0 904790 98 3 (MidNAG)
ISBN 1 85754 344 0 (Carcanet)

The publishers acknowledge financial assistance
from the Arts Council of England and Northern Arts

Set in 10½/12pt Ehrhardt by XL Publishing Services, Tiverton
Printed and bound in England by SRP Ltd, Exeter

Contents

Introduction

Dying of tuberculosis in the City of London Mental Hospital in late 1937, Ivor Gurney was sent the proofs of the forthcoming *Music and Letters* symposium on his life and work. Too ill even to unwrap the parcel, he did not seem to understand its significance. When he was informed by his loyal friend Marion Scott that its appearance had been deliberately timed to coincide with the publication of two volumes of his songs by the Oxford University Press, his only comment was that 'it is too late' (Hurd, p.169). Given his circumstances, Gurney's pessimism was understandable, but it was also somewhat misplaced. His death at the end of the year provoked a flood of obituaries, with newspapers describing him variously as 'England's Schubert' and 'One of Gloucester's Greatest Sons', and both popular and scholarly interest in the man and his work were reawakened. Gerald Finzi, writing to Howard Ferguson after Gurney's funeral, commented bitterly that 'the press has given him in his death more attention in a week than they gave his life in 47 years' (Hurd, p.181), but it was this media interest, fortified by the appearance in January 1938 of both the *Music and Letters* material and the Oxford University Press songs, that began the process of re-establishing Gurney's reputation as a composer. His music was performed again, his songs were broadcast by the BBC and his work at last received the serious critical consideration that it deserved. It was all too late for Gurney himself, of course, but it did ultimately help to restore to prominence one of this century's most intriguing and interesting creative talents.

As welcome as this revaluation was, it nevertheless ignored Gurney's considerable accomplishments as a poet. His contemporaries regarded him primarily as a musician whose published poetry was largely the result of wartime circumstances, and this unfortunate perception was to remain virtually unchallenged for the next forty years. Initially this was partly because so little of Gurney's verse was available, but even when selections from his manuscripts were published – Edmund Blunden's in 1954 and Leonard Clark's in 1973 – the critical and popular response was negligible. It was only in 1978, with the appearance of Michael Hurd's *The Ordeal of Ivor Gurney*, that the tide began to turn. Hurd not only emphasised Gurney's equal commitment to both arts but also provided plentiful examples of previously unpublished poems, creating a consensus amongst reviewers that a new edition of the poetry was needed. Such an edition came four years later with the publication of P. J. Kavanagh's authoritative *Collected Poems of Ivor Gurney*, a selection of almost three hundred poems which at last showed the full range of his poetic achievement and finally established his place in the literary canon.

Placing him exactly, however, remains a matter of some difficulty and depends to some extent on the material available on which to base judgements. For many he takes his place alongside Wilfred Owen, Siegfried Sassoon and Isaac Rosenberg as a poet of the First World War, though his work 'presents a radical revision of conventional ideas about English war poetry' (Featherstone, p.2). Gurney's own reference to himself as 'first war poet of England' (G 52.11.141) reinforces this picture of him, and that role was emphasised by the publication of *War Letters* in 1983 and the republication of *Severn & Somme and War's Embers* four years later. However, Gurney cannot be pigeonholed quite so easily, and his post-war productivity took his poetry in directions which indicate how wrong it is to limit him to being merely a war poet. The publication of two of his asylum collections, *Best Poems and The Book of Five Makings* in 1995, showed the much greater range of his interests. He does indeed write impressively with war as his subject, but he also writes about the Elizabethans, Gloucester, France, London, people and places from his reading and his memory: the inhabitants and geography of his mind.

There is still however the gap between the war years and the productive years after 1922 when Gurney himself gathered much of his poetry into titled collections in the quixotic belief that publication of his poetry would 'save' him from the 'Hell beneath Hell, horror beneath horror' of the asylum (G 52.11.141). But one particular post-war volume does not belong to the asylum years, and, unlike the later volumes that he assembled, it was actually submitted to a publisher as representative of his work of the years from 1919 to 1922. Unfortunately it was rejected, with the result that Gurney unsuccessfully touted it around his contacts in the literary world in the hope that it might find favour elsewhere. Because of his lack of success, poems from this collection have only appeared in print in a piecemeal fashion, in posthumous selections and divorced from the context in which he wished them to appear. Now, for the first time, we are making this collection available to readers in its entirety, allowing us to see the development of his work in the period from the war to the asylum.

Because Gurney gave it no title, we have named it *80 Poems or So*, from his own offhand reference to it in a letter to Marion Scott, where he mentions 'the despatch of a book of verse to Sidgwick, (80 poems or so)' (*Letters*, p.532). The title captures something of the author's character and his attitude towards his text, and we use it to refer to the collection from now on.

80 Poems or So or *Rewards of Wonder*?

It has long been recognised that Gurney prepared a successor to *War's Embers* before his final breakdown, but there has been some doubt as to its identity. Michael Hurd suggests that the collection was called *Rewards of Wonder* and was offered to Sidgwick & Jackson in 1919 but turned down because his earlier book had not been a success. P. J. Kavanagh gives May 1919 as the date of Sidgwick & Jackson's refusal and prints twenty-nine texts under the heading 'From *Rewards of Wonder* (1919-1920)' in his 1982 edition of Gurney's poems. Although he and Hurd disagree slightly on exactly how many poems *Rewards of Wonder* contains – Kavanagh gives a figure of eighty-three whilst Hurd talks of eighty – their broad agreement established *Rewards of Wonder* as the likely representative of Gurney's post-war period, a view reiterated in much subsequent critical discussion of Gurney's poetry.

Hurd and Kavanagh were pioneers and much of the evidence they were working with was fragmentary and ambiguous. Gurney's post-war correspondence frequently dispenses with dates and is often frustratingly vague when it comes to any discussion of his own creative activities, making precise identification of the details of his life in this period difficult. An undated letter from his aunt's house in Longford to his friend and mentor Marion Scott certainly mentions 'the despatch of a book of verse to Sidgwick, (80 poems or so)' and its return, 'sort of rejected but telling me to correct and reject' (*Letters*, p.532). A similar letter to Edmund Blunden – apparently including the material in question – includes the remark that 'Sidgwick with some politeness has rejected it' and asks Blunden to show it to his publisher, Cobden Sanderson (*Letters*, p.539). Other correspondence suggests that both Lascelles Abercrombie and Sir Edward Marsh were similarly approached for help in getting the collection published (*Letters*, p.538 and p.524). Aside from a brief description of the number of texts in the collection and the identification of a poem called 'First Spring' as one of them (*Letters*, p.532 and p.538), Gurney's letters offer little information to help to identify what he submitted or indeed when he submitted it.

Sidgwick & Jackson's correspondence files, now available in the Bodleian Library, help to clarify matters considerably. Marion Scott arranged for the publication of *Severn & Somme* and *War's Embers* on Gurney's behalf and the firm's letters to her, which end in the middle of 1919, do not refer to any successor to *War's Embers* and make no mention of *Rewards of Wonder*. Gurney's name does not appear again in their correspondence for almost three years, when Frank Sidgwick writes to him on 9 May 1922:

> I am sorry to return this MS., but it won't do for publication, for several reasons. First, it is far too long, and the process of selection is your business, not ours. But more important, I cannot help feeling that the poems are unfinished, uncorrected, unpolished as they are certainly unpunctuated. These things should not be left to the reader. I don't care how hard you make the reader's *literary* difficulties, but you must place him in possession of the facts.
>
> Amongst the MSS. received this morning, which you sent with a letter which broke off in the middle of a word and forgot to sign, was a sheet headed 'Midnight' followed by the single line:—
> 'There is no sound within the cottage'
> What are we to make of that? If it is the whole poem, it strikes us as inadequate.
>
> I hope I don't write unsympathetically, but it is so clear that there

is poetry lurking behind your work that it becomes more vexatious to find these brambles across the path. The whole MS. is more like a poet's notebook than a volume of finished poems.

(Sidgwick & Jackson 52, folio 993)

Sidgwick's letter confirms Gurney's account of his approaches to his publishers – later in his letter to Marion Scott, he tells her 'the book according to F. S. S. Sidgwick is more like a poet's note book but O there's good stuff there!' (*Letters*, p.532) – and supplies a definite date for these activities. Later letters confirm that he did indeed 'correct and reject' and then resubmit the material in June, but to little purpose:

I am sorry to return again the MS. 'Forty Poems' but we are unable to see any improvement in it save for a slight reduction in length. The whole thing wears, to us, a haphazard appearance; the true stuff is there, but it doesn't shine out as it should, and much of it seems unmusical. I fear we cannot offer publication.

(Sidgwick & Jackson 53, folio 265)

This correspondence makes clear that Gurney did submit a third collection of '80 poems or so' to Sidgwick & Jackson, but in 1922 and not in 1919. Equally important, it shows that this collection was not *Rewards of Wonder*. If it had a title, either Gurney or Frank Sidgwick would have used it. *Rewards of Wonder* is not named; instead they refer merely to '80 poems' or 'Forty Poems', indicating that its 'haphazard appearance' extended to its not having a title.

Our reassembled volume of *80 Poems or So* bears no direct relation to the only surviving text of *Rewards of Wonder*, although the latter includes alternative versions of three of the poems submitted to Sidgwick & Jackson. *Rewards of Wonder* is in fact another collection made up largely of pre-asylum poetry that Gurney intermittently corrected and revised from late 1921 until late 1924. It now exists only in the form of an incomplete typescript produced at the request of Ralph Vaughan Williams in 1943 and, although Gurney listed it as one of '7 Books' that he wanted 'to publish. To get Editors to print' in an asylum appeal written in August 1923 (G 52.11.137), it was never sent to a publisher. The material offered to Sidgwick & Jackson in 1922, on the other hand, represents what Gurney regarded as the best of what he had written since the publication of *War's Embers* three years earlier. Some of the poems it contains were completed as early as 1919 and the presence of these alongside his later work seems to be an attempt on Gurney's part to allow the reader to trace his remarkable poetic development during this period. As Sidgwick's description of what he received suggests, Gurney was evidently unwell by the time he came to make his selection and it can thus be seen as a last desperate attempt to place his work in front of the public before his condition overwhelmed him – 'an unsuccessful and angry poet writing to a successful poet who has already done things for him', as he described himself in one of his letters to Edmund Blunden (*Letters*, p.539).

Identifying *80 Poems or So*
In reconstructing *80 Poems or So* we have drawn on material from three distinct sources to make up the 86 poems which we believe it contained. Seventy-two of them are typewritten copies made by Dorothy Gurney. Writing to his Gloucester friend John Haines in June 1923, Gurney's younger sister Dorothy identifies herself as the typist of the material submitted to Sidgwick & Jackson a year earlier. She also notes – and this is important for our treatment of the texts – that what she produced was 'unfinished', often 'incomprehensible' and 'without punctuation' (G 84.14). One group of miscellaneous poems in the Gurney Archive is prefaced by a note which reads 'THE TYPED COPIES on thin paper appear to have been made by Dorothy Gurney' (G 19.103); amongst these is a typescript on very thin paper of 'First Spring', the poem identified by Gurney as part of his rejected collection in his correspondence with Marion Scott and Edmund Blunden in 1922 (*Letters*, pp. 532 and 538). This particular typescript is thus part of his submission to Sidgwick & Jackson, and the same provenance can be ascribed to other typescripts and carbon-copies in the Gurney Archive produced on the same typewriter on the same thin paper in the same typing style. Once retrieved from their disparate locations in the Archive, these texts form a collection of seventy-two

individual poems, some of which are indeed 'unfinished', 'uncorrected' and 'unpunctuated'. Others are significantly revised, repunctuated and marked by Gurney with the letter A or B for inclusion in his revised selection.

The single-line text of 'Midnight' that Frank Sidgwick found so problematic is not amongst these typescripts. However, it does appear amongst a group of manuscripts on long sheets of lined paper, again marked for selection by Gurney with either an A or a B. These manuscripts represent part of the copy-text used by Dorothy Gurney for the creation of her brother's submission, though her typescripts of the twelve poems which they contain are no longer extant. That these texts once formed part of Gurney's *80 poems or So* is reinforced by the presence of typed copies of poems from this group in a set described as 'MISCELLANEOUS POEMS Sent to Mr Edward Marsh by Ivor Gurney (with the Three Manuscript Books) in September 1922' (G 19.103). We have supplied the text of 'Midnight' from a manuscript source.

Dorothy's other copy-texts – mostly pages torn from exercise books and other loose sheets of paper – survive only in a fragmentary state, but one red 'Ayliffe' brand hard-cover exercise book has survived in its entirety and supplies a number of versions which she transcribed. One of its texts has been marked for copying but no typescript exists. Adding this text to the material already assembled produces a collection of eighty-six poems, the 'thundering good stuff' of which Gurney was so proud (*Letters*, p.539).

A history of *80 Poems or So*

It would perhaps be useful at this point to trace the history of the creation and subsequent fate of *80 Poems or So*. When Gurney travelled to Cornwall in 1918 to spend Christmas as the guest of the novelist Ethel Voynich, he took with him a small green pocket notebook in which he recorded his impressions of the landscape and ideas and sketches for poems. Returning to London to resume his studies at the Royal College of Music at the start of 1919, he developed the material in this notebook into completed poems and then transferred them on to individual sheets of lined paper. Writing to John Haines on

16 January 1919, he comments on having 'one set of verses in rough; another half done' (*Letters*, p.472) and sending Marion Scott some new poems a month later, he goes so far as to suggest that 'Book three you see is in the making!' (*Letters*, p.474). Some of these drafts found their way into the red 'Ayliffe' exercise book, where they were further revised. In July, encouraged perhaps by the publication of two of his poems in *The Spectator* earlier in the year and wishing to test the waters for his 'Book three', he chose a number of texts from this note-book and submitted them with material from his 'verses in rough' to five journals – *Harper's Magazine*, *The Century*, *The Spectator*, *The New Witness* and *The Athenaeum*.

Gurney moved from London to High Wycombe in September and it was here that he heard that none of his submissions had been successful. Reporting the news to John Haines, his tone was light-hearted – 'My pet malediction on the whole!' (*Letters*, p.492) – but this failure, accompanied by the knowledge that sales of *War's Embers* were not going well, must have been a blow to him; he reported to Marion Scott soon afterwards, that the editor of *The London Mercury*, J. C. Squire, had described him as 'the best of the young men below the horizon' and then added bitterly: 'which led to a natural question as to why he had rejected so much lately' (*Letters*, p.497). In the following year, however, he had two poems apiece accepted by *Music and Letters* and *The Royal College of Music Magazine* and this seems to have spurred him in October 1920 into sending the red exercise book to Edmund Blunden, at that time the Assistant Editor of *The Athenaeum*. It was in his possession for over three months – replying to an enquiry from John Haines in February 1921, Gurney offered to 'ask Blunden about the red M.S. book' (*Letters*, p.508) – but Blunden eventually decided against publishing any of its contents and returned it to its author. Two months later, Gurney gave up all pretence of being a student at the Royal College of Music and returned to Gloucestershire, moving in with his aunt at 1 Westfield Terrace in Longford and finding occasional employment as a farm labourer. Unsuited to manual work, unable to publish his poems, desperately short of money and increasingly disturbed by physical and mental illness, his prospects were now bleak indeed.

Despite his circumstances, the remainder of 1921 was a period of great productivity for Gurney. He spent the summer drafting poems 'in shoals. Jolly good some' (*Letters*, p.516) in a school exercise book and on long sheets of lined paper. By the end of the year, he had begun to revise and transcribe many of these into two hard-cover exercise books, one bound in black and the other in green. Two short-lived posts as a cinema pianist in Bude and Plumstead over Christmas and the New Year did not retard his progress and he was soon filling a new pink marbled hard-cover exercise book with revisions of earlier material and new poems. With his long-abandoned 'Book three' once again in mind, he spent the beginning of 1922 selecting the material that he felt best represented his previous three years' work, favouring those poems which had already been published in periodicals. Interestingly enough, he ignored the contents of his current notebooks and returned instead to the red 'Ayliffe' exercise book and his 'shoals' of poems, tearing appropriate texts from the school exercise book and marking others in his loose manuscripts and the 'Ayliffe' notebook with a series of letters and crosses. Despite the haphazard state of some of this material, it was handed over to Dorothy Gurney for typing and in May submitted to Sidgwick & Jackson.

Sidgwick & Jackson's first refusal prompted Gurney into sending *80 Poems or So* to Lascelles Abercrombie, who replied with 'a very nice letter about my things' (*Letters*, p.538). He also revised the collection, reducing it to half of its original length by following his usual practice of lettering favourite poems and correcting those which remained. This amended version was resubmitted in the second week of June but rejected a fortnight later. Stung by this refusal, Gurney then sent the rejected collection to Edmund Blunden for his opinion. By this time, however, his personal situation had worsened considerably. Efforts made on his behalf by Walter de la Mare and Sir Edward Marsh had provided him with a job at Gloucester Tax Office but his rapidly deteriorating mental state meant that he was unable to keep it for long. Moving in uninvited with his brother Ronald, he made repeated suicide attempts, believing that 'electrical tricks' were being played on him. In September, in a final desperate attempt to see his work in print, he despatched *80 Poems or So* and the three hard-cover exercise books to Marsh, apologising for 'the horrible state of some of it' but explaining that he was 'pretty badly done nowadays' (*Letters*, p.524). By the end of the month, he was certified insane by two local doctors and committed to Barnwood House, a private asylum just outside Gloucester. At the end of the year, he was moved to the City of London Mental Hospital at Dartford, which was to be his home until his death in 1937.

The fate of *80 Poems or So* from this point onwards is somewhat confused. Hearing of Gurney's breakdown, Marsh sent all the poems he had received to Marion Scott (G 19.3) but it seems that *80 Poems or So* was passed on to Gurney's mother by June 1923 – Dorothy Gurney's letter to John Haines, enclosing the typescripts, notes that 'this other collection' was retrieved from her (G 84.14). Thereafter it was either in the possession of John Haines or Marion Scott; texts from it formed part of her selection for the abortive Gollancz edition of 1928. It seems to have been available to Edmund Blunden when he made his selection during the early 1950s; certainly, his practice of removing particular typescripts that he wanted to use from their original groupings affected the collection's present state, as did Joy Finzi's reorganisation of the Gurney Archive in the 1960s. By gathering together variant texts of individual poems as she did, it became possible to understand the development of particular texts but at the cost of obscuring their original arrangement. At present, Dorothy Gurney's typescripts are scattered throughout the Gurney Archive in over a dozen different locations.

The Contents of *80 Poems or So*

80 Poems or So is fascinating because it lies at a crucial juncture not only in the development of Gurney's poetry but also in the development of English poetry as a whole. One suspects that his publishers' rejection was the result not merely of the untidiness but also the strangeness of the content of Gurney's projected volume; he was pushing poetry in ways that not every publisher or reader of poetry would be able to follow. Of course, he was not the only poet to write and wish to publish unconventional poetry at that time; his manuscript was submitted in the year which saw the publication of T. S.

Eliot's *The Waste Land*, a poem traditionally seen as not only establishing the aesthetic and cultural importance of Modernism but also sounding the death-knell of the Georgian movement.

In truth, the Georgians were already in decline and had been for some time, with poor sales and a lukewarm critical response convincing Sir Edward Marsh that *Georgian Poetry 1920-1922* would be the last volume in the series. Whilst J. C. Squire's efforts to sustain the remnants of the movement in the pages of *The London Mercury* maintained their popularity amongst the general public, it was the adherents of Modernism who came to be seen as the most significant figures of the period. Accordingly, Gurney's strong affiliations with the Georgians – he knew many of them personally and frequently set their poems to music – undoubtedly prejudiced both contemporary and subsequent responses to his work. Both *Severn & Somme* and *War's Embers*, with their easy lyricism and rural concerns, look like Georgian texts on a superficial reading and, given that so little of his later poetry was available during his lifetime, it is small wonder that he has traditionally been placed among the Georgians. All this might have been different if Sidgwick & Jackson had chosen to accept *80 Poems or So*, or if Gurney had submitted the volume to a less traditional publisher.

Technically, the contents of the collection represent a significant advance on the material in his two earlier books. Whilst some of the older poems have the uneasy combination of Georgian facility and idiosyncratic ruggedness that was a quality of his earlier verse, the newer poems reveal the existence of two distinctive yet complementary poetic styles. Gurney can, when he wishes, write in a straightforward, fluent way – the colloquial lyricism so prized by many of the first wave of Georgian poets like Wilfrid Gibson and Rupert Brooke – but he also has the confidence to allow his own individual voice to carry the weight of a poem when the occasion demands it. Profoundly influenced not only by Whitman but also by the rhythms, syntax and language of Elizabethan and Jacobean playwrights and poets such as Jonson, Webster and Tourneur, he creates a unique poetic discourse that combines Georgian concerns with the kind of linguistic allusiveness and difficulty favoured by the Modernists. Strictly speaking, he belongs in neither camp – he is far too idiosyncratic for that – but *80*

Poems or So offers a tantalising glimpse of how Georgian poetry could have reinvented itself and challenged the aesthetic supremacy of Modernism in this period. This is the work of someone consciously determined to create a new kind of English poetry.

With this new confidence comes an expansion of his themes, though it should first be remarked that there is a curious silence about the war. Writing to Marion Scott in June of 1922, Gurney reported that 'I write War Poems. (rather bad.)' (*Letters*, p.540), and the war was henceforth to be a central feature of his poetry. But in the interlude marked by *80 Poems or So* his interests are elsewhere, particularly in what he terms 'realty'. This word focuses attention on the physical world of the present, and indicates Gurney's relationship to other poetic movements. Walter Pater – whom we know Gurney read – had said that 'the first condition of the poetic way of seeing and presenting things is particularisation' (Pater, p.208); and Pound had given as one part of the 'Imagist Triad' the 'Direct treatment of the "thing" whether subjective or objective' (Pound, p.3). Gurney incorporates this directness within his own vision.

He almost certainly discovered the term in the poetry of Gerard Manley Hopkins, though it is also a legal term and might have been found in the wills of his father or Margaret Hunt, both of whom had recently died. Haines remembered how in 'those early days after the War' he had lent Gurney 'the books he desired to read, books which brought him in touch with the work of Edward Thomas and Gerard Manley Hopkins, the two modern poets he most admired and those who contributed most to his literary technique' (Haines, p.63). In 'Duns Scotus's Oxford' Hopkins calls Scotus 'Of realty the rarest-veinèd unraveller', and Gurney picks up the term and in 'Fragment' forcefully expresses the need to explore the 'taste of Realty':

> Realty has never margin for desire,
> And matter's the true business of the soul.

'On a Town' also asks

> Who could be faithful to a dream delight
> When realty holds so strong the actual hour?

80 Poems or So is full of recognition of the significance of mundane, everyday things. 'The Garden' celebrates not 'that ink-proud lady the rose' but 'ordered curly and plain cabbages', whilst 'Common Things' is a panegyric on 'the whole family of crockery', 'the touch, smell, feel of paper' and 'old pipes / Gone warped in service'. He feels that it is the poet's role to celebrate what might be overlooked, especially if it is transitory. In 'The Town', for example, he commemorates 'homely cities' as something to be 'downnoted in a book, / Before progress has marched them out of door', whilst in 'Change', he regrets the way 'bright potato leaves' have displaced 'Grain . . . so noble' in the landscape, celebrating what has been lost in the hope that it will make people 'regret what poets may sing'. His verse becomes both a means of preserving such things and a way of drawing attention to them in all their common beauty.

If Gurney is aware of man-made alterations to the countryside, then he is also aware of natural changes and his poetry becomes an attempt to capture and celebrate these too. In 'Moments' he regrets that 'the Autumn goes beyond my pen' but poems such as 'Coming Dusk' and 'Now are the hills born new' find subjects not 'beyond his pen', recording for posterity moments of transition when the landscape is at its most sublime. Poems such as 'Near Redmarley' and 'Generations' reveal an awareness of the historical continuity that underlies such changes – another of Gurney's primary concerns in this collection – but here again there is a sense of Gurney trying to commemorate what might be overlooked. Not merely content with contrasting his county's attractions with the desolation of France or London's bleakness, he instead explores the processes that go to make up those attractions. Gloucestershire's rivers, roads, bridges, even its inhabitants all come under his gaze, to be faithfully recreated in his poems through a language that complements its subject and becomes part of the texture of the poem's meaning. Confident that he has at last found the ability to express himself fully, he can now write about the intricacies of experience with assurance.

If realty is an important element in these poems, it is enriched by Gurney's ability to recognise the mythical potential of the everyday. North Woolwich puts him in mind of Ancient Greece, 'that ugly, that

evil smelling / Township' showing the potential for transformation
into something more beautiful as he gazes upon it. Gloucestershire
becomes peopled with figures from myth and literature in 'Personages'
and 'Generations'. The literary and historical inheritance of England
lie close to the surface for Gurney and his poems liberate these
elements to create a vision of national identity that combines the mate-
rial with the transcendental, turning farmers into gods and the land-
scape into Elizabethan theatres. Shakespeare, as ever, is the presiding
literary deity in these matters but it is a Shakespeare mediated through
Gurney's consciousness, Shakespeare the working writer, Shakes-
peare the deer-poacher and teacher, not Shakespeare the vague
symbolic figurehead of national identity. If Gurney's debt to the
Elizabethans for their linguistic and stylistic resources is a large one,
then it is adequately repaid in his celebration of them as vital, living
components of daily life.

His poetry attempts to fuse these perceptions of realty and myth, to
find the actual details which simultaneously involve the eternal truths,
as in his picture of 'North Woolwich' where he envisages an almost
pre-Raphaelite Christ as 'A foreman carpenter not yet full grown'.
The landscape and history of Gloucestershire are, for Gurney, not
merely praiseworthy in their own right but also as paradigms of
Englishness. Eschewing the facile equation between Nature and
Nation, he recognises that England is not just a collection of bucolic
fantasies but a real, material location which mixes the urban with the
rural, the past with the present and the good with the bad. His fasci-
nation with cities in general can be traced back to this perception, and
it is London in particular which stimulates his most subtle and
surprising responses. Gurney's London is not Eliot's 'unreal city' but
rather a city of realty made up of social activity, geographical detail and
historical survival; yet its recreation as an imaginative space in his
poems frequently echoes the Modernist idea of the City as a place of
myth and mire.

It is London, too, which reveals his reluctance to accept other
aspects of the static versions of Englishness espoused by his contem-
poraries. 'The Road' may describe the capital of England and thus
symbolise the nation, yet for him it also epitomises the racially

mercurial nature of national identity - London belongs not only to the 'pale-faced' indigenous population but also to 'Jewesses / And Poles and Russ'. Similarly, the English countryside is realised not merely in terms of rolling hills, quaint customs and tradition but as a living human environment with its fair share of poverty and distress. Man-made changes to the landscape are realised in terms of their social cost and it is the 'out-of-work' who carry on elver-fishing in bad weather when others have departed in 'Rainy Midnight'. These kinds of perceptions, this willingness to see beyond traditionally monolithic ideas of nation, its mythical and historical patinas, its topographical identities, are what makes *80 Poems or So* such a challenging volume and show just how far removed from his contemporaries Gurney was by this stage in his career.

Editing *80 Poems or So*

Had *80 Poems or So* been accepted for publication in 1922, it would have caused problems for its editors. The special circumstances of the war had made it easy for Marion Scott to take a decisive role as editor for *Severn & Somme* – even the choice of title was, as Gurney wrote to her, 'your business' (*Letters*, p.288). But Gurney soon found himself unable to resist the temptation to rewrite almost every time he saw a manuscript or typescript. Even J. C. Squire, the staunchest of his supporters in the London literary world, was reluctant to send him proofs in case he felt the need to 'muck them about too much' (G 5.12.3). Instead, Squire chose silently to amend those things in Gurney's poems that he felt were 'incapable of explanation' (G 5.12.2).

We do not wish to be as intrusive as Squire, but it is evident that we had to take a firm editorial hand. Frank Sidgwick's account of the raw material for this book gives some idea of the state of our copy-text, and it would obviously be foolish to reproduce the errors of spelling and transcription that Dorothy Gurney was all too aware might be present – as she wrote to John Haines, Ivor 'sent them on without even checking my typing, in which I felt sure I had made "howlers" in reading his writing' (G 84.14). But, whilst avoiding bringing a ragged Gurney before the public, we have also been careful not to destroy the rugged Gurney in the process and our editorial intervention has involved only minor changes. We have standardised the form of Gurney's titles. We have replaced his double inverted commas with single ones throughout. We have regularised his spelling – using his preferred form of 'gray' for 'grey', for example – and restored his habitual capitalisation of the names of seasons. When we encountered obvious transcription errors on Dorothy Gurney's part, we have sought readings based on surviving manuscript evidence wherever possible. The major copy-text has been Dorothy Gurney's typescripts on which we have based the substantives; but where there is a manuscript version, its accidentals have often been preferred. We have lightly punctuated some of Gurney's more linguistically obscure passages, bearing in mind at all times that the typescript might be the nearest evidence we have of Gurney's often rhetorical punctuation.

Our main intrusion into the text is that we have given it a title and an order. There is no way of knowing whether its contents had a specific arrangement, and we have accordingly felt free to group the poems in a way which reflects Gurney's areas of interest in this period: the seasons and their effect on both landscape and observer; the natural aesthetics of light and dark; London and its sights and crowds; Gloucestershire and its topography; the intrusion of the mythic and literary into the material world; realty and the realisation of the material world; and finally Gurney's reflections upon life and poetic vocation. These categories are not rigid – Gurney may touch on several in the same poem – but we hope we have created a structure which not only reflects his immediate concerns but also suggests those areas of interest that permeate all of his work. Our editorial aim has been to present this material as it might have appeared before Gurney's contemporaries, so that modern readers have the opportunity to appreciate what he described as its 'beauty and a very good sense of form, and no swank' (*Letters*, p.539).

Texts Cited

Featherstone   *War Poetry: An Introductory Reader*, edited by Simon
                Featherstone (Routledge, 1995).

G   unpublished material deposited in the Gurney
                Archive, Gloucester Library, with its location
                number.

Haines   John Haines, 'An Hour With Books', *The Gloucester
                Journal*, 5 January 1935, p.28. Reprinted in *The Ivor
                Gurney Society Journal*, vol. 1 (1995), pp.61–5.

Hurd   Michael Hurd, *The Ordeal of Ivor Gurney* (Oxford
                University Press, 1978).

Letters   *Ivor Gurney: Collected Letters*, edited by R. K. R.
                Thornton (MidNAG/Carcanet, 1991).

Pater   Walter Pater, *Appreciations* (Macmillan, 1901).

Pound   Ezra Pound, *Literary Essays of Ezra Pound* (Faber
                and Faber, 1954).

Suggested Further Reading

Ivor Gurney, *Severn and Somme* (Sidgwick & Jackson, 1917).

—*War's Embers* (Sidgwick & Jackson, 1919).

—*Poems by Ivor Gurney*, Principally Selected from Unpublished Manuscripts with a Memoir by Edmund Blunden (Hutchinson, 1954).

—*Poems of Ivor Gurney 1890-1937*, with an Introduction by Edmund Blunden and a Bibliographical Note by Leonard Clark (Chatto & Windus, 1973).

—*Collected Poems of Ivor Gurney*, Chosen, Edited and with an Introduction by P. J. Kavanagh (Oxford University Press, 1982).

—*Severn & Somme and War's Embers*, edited by R. K. R. Thornton (MidNAG/Carcanet, 1987).

—*Ivor Gurney: Selected Poems*, Selected and Introduced by P. J. Kavanagh (Oxford University Press, 1990).

—*Ivor Gurney: Collected Letters*, edited by R. K. R. Thornton (MidNAG/Carcanet, 1991).

—*Best Poems and The Book of Five Makings*, edited by R. K. R. Thornton and George Walter (MidNAG/Carcanet, 1995).

—*Everyman's Poetry: Ivor Gurney*, selected and edited by George Walter (Everyman, 1996).

The Ivor Gurney Society Journal, vols 1–3 (1995–7).

Geoffrey Hill, 'Gurney's Hobby', *Essays in Criticism*, vol. 34, no. 2, (April 1984), pp.97–128.

Andrew Motion, 'Beaten Down Continually', *Times Literary Supplement*, no. 4150 (15 October 1982), p.1121.

Marion Scott *et al*, 'Ivor Gurney', *Music and Letters*, vol. XIX, no. 1 (January 1938).

R.K.R. Thornton and George Walter *Ivor Gurney: Towards a Bibliography* (The Ivor Gurney Society and the School of English at the University of Birmingham, 1996).

George Walter, 'Loose Women and Lonely Lambs: The Rise and Fall of Georgian Poetry', *British Poetry 1900–1950*, edited by Gary Day and Brian Docherty (Macmillan, 1995), pp.14–36.

Acknowledgements

We would like to thank Penny Ely, the Trustee of the Gurney Estate, for permission to publish these poems. The originals are in the Gurney Archive at the Gloucester Library and we are grateful to the staff there for their unfailing help and interest. We are also grateful to Linda Coode and the Gloucester City Museum and Art Gallery for permission to reproduce the picture on the cover, and to the Bodleian Library for permission to print Frank Sidgwick's letters to Gurney. Thanks are due to Harry Buglass for preparing the map, and our personal thanks are offered to Anne Johnson, Val Davison, Fuyubi Nakamura and Catherine Gibb.

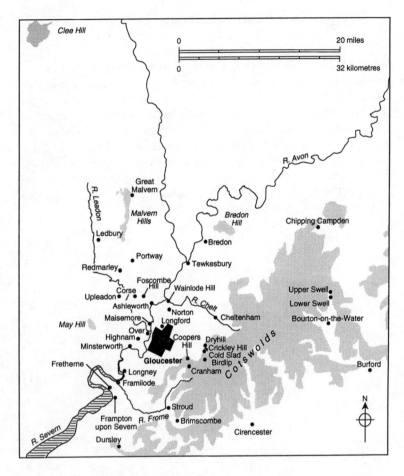

Gurney's Gloucester and Cotswolds

Chronology

This Chronology makes minor corrections to previous accounts of Gurney's life and emphasises his creative activities and publications. Titles of individual poems are in inverted commas, whilst titles of individual songs, song cycles and collections of poetry are in italics.

1890

28 August   Ivor Bertie Gurney born at 3 Queen Street, Gloucester, the son of David Gurney, a tailor, and Florence Lugg. He is the second of four surviving children: Winifred, born in 1886, Ronald, born in 1894, and Dorothy, born in 1900. Alfred Hunter Cheesman, the curate at All Saints' Church, acts as godfather at his christening. The family move to 19 Barton Street, house and shop, shortly after Gurney's birth.

1896   Attends the National School and All Saints' Sunday School. The Gurney family purchase a piano.

1899   Joins the choir of All Saints' Church.

1900   Wins a place in Gloucester Cathedral Choir and starts attending the King's School, where he learns the organ.

1904   Sings with Madame Albani at the Three Choirs Festival and begins to write music.

1905   Begins close association with Canon Cheesman and Margaret and Emily Hunt, all of whom encourage his creative talents.

1906   Leaves the Cathedral Choir and the King's School to become an articled pupil of Dr Herbert Brewer, the organist of Gloucester Cathedral. Makes friends with Herbert Howells, a fellow pupil of Brewer's, F. W. Harvey and John Haines. Works temporarily as an organist at Whitminster, Hempsted and the Mariners' Church in Gloucester's Docklands.

1907   Passes the matriculation examination for Durham University.

1911   Wins an open scholarship for composition at the Royal College of Music of £40 per annum, with Cheesman providing another £40. Takes digs in Fulham. Taught composition by Charles Villiers Stanford and makes friends with Marion M. Scott and Ethel Voynich.

1912   Howells wins a composition scholarship to the Royal College of Music. He and Gurney form a friendship with another new student, Arthur Benjamin.

1913   Begins to write poetry.
May   Diagnosed as suffering from dyspepsia and 'neurasthenia' by Dr Harper and returns to Gloucestershire to recuperate.
Winter   Writes his settings of five Elizabethan lyrics, 'The Elizas'.

1914
August   Volunteers for military service but is rejected because of his defective eyesight.
October   Takes a post as organist at Christ Church, High Wycombe, where he makes the acquaintance of the

Chapman family. Falls in love with Kitty Chapman and asks for permission to marry her, but it is refused.

1915

9 February

Volunteers again and is drafted into the 5th Gloucester Reserve Battalion, the '2/5th Glosters'. Spends the rest of the year in training at Northampton, Chelmsford and Epping.

August

Begins to send Marion Scott his poems and rediscovers the poetry of Walt Whitman, writing to Ethel Voynich that 'he has taken me like a flood'.

December

'Afterwards' and 'To the Poet Before Battle' published in *The Royal College of Music Magazine*.

1916

February

2/5th Glosters move to Tidworth and then on to Park House Camp on Salisbury Plain.

25 May

Arrives in Le Havre and is sent into trenches at Riez Bailleul.

8 June

Moves on to Laventie.

15 June

Relieves the 2nd/1st Bucks in the Fauquissart-Laventie sector. Billeted at La Gorgue .

July

'To Certain Comrades' published in *The Royal College of Music Magazine*.

19 July

Placed in reserve for the attack on Aubers Ridge and 'on Rest' at Richebourg, Neuve-Chappelle, Robecq and Gonnehem.

28 August

Admitted to a Casualty Clearing Station to have his teeth attended to.

27 October

Battalion moves south to Albert and the Somme sector.

December

Sent to a Rest Station with 'a cold in the stomach' and then takes a temporary job with the water carts in the Sanitary Section at 61st Divisional Headquarters.

1917

7 January	Returns to normal duties.
15 February	2/5th Glosters moved to the Ablaincourt sector.
18 March	Battalion follows the German withdrawal to Caulaincourt and then on to Vermand.
7 April	Wounded on Good Friday in the upper arm and sent to hospital at the 55th Infantry Base Depot, Rouen.
18 May	Back with Battalion, which moves to the Arras Front.
23 June	2/5th Glosters 'on Rest' at Buire-au-Bois. Becomes platoon's crack shot.
July	'Song of Pain and Beauty' published in *The Royal College of Music Magazine*.
14 July	Sidgwick & Jackson agree to publish Gurney's poems.
15 July	Transfers to the 184 Machine Gun Company at Vaux.
31 July	In reserve for the battle of Passchendaele. Battalion moves on to Buysscheure.
10 September	Gassed at St Julien.
25 September	Arrives at the Edinburgh War Hospital, Bangour, where he meets and falls in love with Annie Nelson Drummond, a VAD nurse. Their relationship does not last.
November	'Strange Service', 'Afterwards', 'To Certain Comrades' and 'To the Poet Before Battle' are published in E. B. Osborn's anthology *The Muse in Arms*.
	Transferred to Seaton Delaval for a signalling course. *Severn & Somme* published.

1918

12 February	Granted leave to visit his sick father.
25 February	Examined for the effects of gas and admitted to Newcastle General Hospital.

March	Moved to Brancepeth Castle, a convalescent depot.
28 March	Writes to Marion Scott telling her that he has spoken to 'the spirit of Beethoven', clearly a sign of some kind of nervous breakdown.
April	'Ypres' and 'After Music' published in *The Royal College of Music Magazine*.
22 April	Returns to Newcastle General Hospital and is then moved on to Seaton Delaval.
8 May	Sent to Lord Derby's War Hospital, Warrington. Hospitals in the area are pioneering the use of 'Faradisation' – controlled electrical charges – as a treatment for shell-shock, though there is no evidence of its use on Gurney.
June	'The Immortal Hour' published in *The Westminster Gazette*.
19 June	Sends a suicide note to Marion Scott and tells his superiors that he hears voices and wishes to be sent to an asylum.
4 July	Sent to Middlesex War Hospital in St Albans.
4 October	Discharged from the army with a pension of 12 shillings a week. Not granted a full pension because his condition is 'aggravated but not caused by' the war. Returns to 19 Barton Street, Gloucester.
October	Working in a munitions factory and worrying his friends and family with his erratic behaviour. Makes several attempts to go to sea. The Chapman family offer to adopt him, but his own family do not allow this.
11 November	Finishes work at the munitions factory.
7 December	'The Battalion is Now "On Rest"' published in *The Spectator*.
Christmas	Goes to stay with Ethel Voynich in Cornwall, taking the green pocket book with him.

1919

January	Returns to the Royal College of Music, where Ralph Vaughan Williams is his composition teacher. Moves into digs in West Kensington and writes to John Haines that he has 'one set of verses in rough; another half done'. *Severn & Somme* reprinted.
11 January	'In a Ward' published in *The Spectator*. 'The Day of Victory' published in *The Gloucester Journal*.
22 February	'The Volunteer' published in *The Spectator*.
25 February	Returns to 19 Barton Street to correct the proofs of *War's Embers*, his second volume for Sidgwick & Jackson. Tells Marion Scott: 'Book three you see is in the making!'
3 March	Margaret Hunt dies.
22 April	Working at Dryhill Farm, Shurdington
May	Living in St John's Wood, London, and using the red 'Ayliffe' hard-cover notebook. *War's Embers* published.
10 May	His father, David Gurney, dies.
August	Submits poems from his 'set of verses in rough' and the red 'Ayliffe' notebook to *The Century*, *The Athenaeum*, *Harper's Magazine*, *The New Witness* and *The Spectator*. Goes on a walking tour of the Black Mountains with John Haines, moving to High Wycombe on his return.
September	Takes a post as organist at Christ Church, High Wycombe and learns that none of his poems have been accepted.
October	Moving in London literary circles but suffering from 'nerves and an inability to think or write at all clearly'.
8 November	Visits John Masefield at Boar's Hill, Oxford, with F. W. Harvey.

1920

Late February   Walks from High Wycombe to Dryhill Farm via Oxford.

March   *The Twa Corbies* published in *Music and Letters.*

May   Tries to set up home in a cottage at Cold Slad, Dryhill.

July   Stainer & Bell publish *Captain Stratton's Fancy.* Winthrop Rogers publish 'The Elizas' – *Orpheus, Sleep, Tears, Spring* and *Under the Greenwood Tree.* Boosey & Co. publish *Carol of the Skiddaw Yowes.* 'The Hooligan' and 'April 20th 1919' published in *The Royal College of Music Magazine.*

October   Living in lodgings in Earls Court, London. 'Equal Mistress' and 'The Crocus Ring' published in *Music and Letters.*

6 November   Receives a Government Grant of £120 a year, backdated to 25 September. Meets Edmund Blunden and Wilfrid Gibson.

18 December   *Desire in Spring* published in *The Chapbook.*

1921

    Chappell & Co. publish *West Sussex Drinking Song.* Boosey & Co. publish *I will go with my father a-ploughing.*

12 February   'Fine Rain' published in *The Nation.*

March   Boosey & Co. publish *Since thou, O fondest and truest.*

April   Living with his aunt at 1 Westfield Terrace, Longford, Gloucester. Tries unsuccessfully to get his poems included in Edward Marsh's anthology *Georgian Poetry 1920-1922.* Looks for and eventually finds work on a farm.

May   'Song of Pain and Beauty' and 'To the Poet Before Battle' reprinted in J. C. Squire's *Selections from Modern Poets.*

June–July   Living at the Five Alls, Stokenchurch, near High

	Wycombe.
Late July	Formally leaves the Royal College of Music and returns to his aunt's house in Longford, writing to Marion Scott that 'something is more wrong than formerly' but that 'Poems have got done in shoals. Jolly good some'.
August	Works in a cold storage depot in Southwark for a fortnight and then returns to Longford, finding employment on a farm.
20 August	'Western Sky' published in *The Nation and Athenaeum*.
September	Describes himself as 'not yet well'. Winthrop Rogers publish *The Bonnie Earl of Murray* and *The County Mayo*.
October	Probably using both the green hard-cover notebook and the black hard-cover notebook by this time. Winthrop Rogers publish the *Five Preludes for Piano*.
December	Obtains a post playing the piano at a cinema in Bude but is retained for only a week.

1922

	Stainer & Bell publish *Edward, Edward*. Boosey & Co. publish *Come, O come my Life's delight*.
January	Living in Walham Green, London, and probably using the pink marbled hard-cover notebook by this time.
7 January	'This City' published in *The Gloucester Journal*.
Mid January	Moves to Plumstead, London. Finds a job playing the piano in a cinema there but is retained only for a fortnight.
February	Returns to his aunt's house in Longford and finds work on a farm. Selects the best of the poems that he has written over the past three years and gives them to Dorothy Gurney to type.
15 April	'On a Two Hundredth Birthday' published in *The*

Gloucester Journal.

May	Looks for a job in the Civil Service. Submits a collection of '80 poems or so' taken from the type-scripts produced by his sister to Sidgwick & Jackson. They return it, advising him to reduce and revise its contents, and it is passed to Lascelles Abercrombie for his comments.
10 June	Resubmits a corrected and shortened version of his '80 poems or so' to Sidgwick & Jackson but it is rejected again. 'Tewkesbury' published in *The Gloucester Journal.*
July	Sends his rejected collection to Edmund Blunden in the hope that he will pass them on to his publisher, Cobden Sanderson. Now writing 'War poems. (rather bad.)'. 'The Springs of Music', an essay, published in *The Musical Quarterly.*
3 July	Begins work at the Gloucester Tax Office but loses his post after twelve weeks.
September	Moves in univited with his brother Ronald and his wife at 52 Worcester Street, Gloucester. Behaviour very disturbed and he makes a number of suicide attempts. Sends his '80 poems or so' accompanied by 'Three Manuscript Books' – presumably the black, green and pink marbled hard-cover note-books – to Sir Edward Marsh in another attempt to see his poems in print.
Late September	Friends try to arrange treatment at a Convalescent Home near Bristol.
28 September	Certified insane by Dr Soutar and Dr Terry and is admitted to Barnwood House, a private asylum near Gloucester.
October	'Encounters' and 'The March Past' published in *The London Mercury.*
21 October	Escapes but is recaptured after a few hours.
8 November	Escapes again but is recaptured at a police station.
21 December	Transferred to the City of London Mental

Hospital at Dartford – known by him as 'Stone House' or 'Dr Steen's' – and comes under the care of Dr Robinson, the Second Assistant Medical Officer.

1923

Stainer & Bell publish the song cycle *Ludlow and Teme* as part of the Carnegie Collection of British Music and *Five Western Watercolours*.

January	'Sights' published in *The London Mercury*.
6 January	Escapes whilst walking in the hospital grounds and travels to London. Visits J. C. Squire and Ralph Vaughan Williams, who informs the authorities. Recaptured and returned to Dartford via Hounslow Infirmary.
February	Physical condition improves but mental condition remains the same.
31 March	'The Road' published in *The Spectator*.
May	'Advice' published in *The London Mercury*.
June	Ronald Gurney sends his brother's manuscripts to Marion Scott. Dorothy Gurney sends her typescripts to John Haines, who is also gathering material.
August	Treated with 'Malarial injections', which have no effect on his mental state.
Christmas	Entertains his fellow-patients with his piano-playing during the festivities.

1924

January	Receives seven visits from Dr Cyriax, an osteopath, for treatment for pains in his neck and head. 'Thoughts of New England', 'New Year's Eve', 'Old Tale', 'The Cloud', 'Smudgy Dawn', 'Tobacco' and 'Brimscombe' published in *The London Mercury*.
March	Refuses to get up from his bed on the verandah.

Mental condition worsens.

July Contribution to 'Charles Villiers Stanford. By Some of His Pupils' published in *Music and Letters*.

August Sends out a number of appeals listing seven new books of poems and whom they have been sent to: *Roman gone East* is apparently with Arthur Benjamin, *Fatigues and Magnificences* is with his old army companion Basil Cridlan and Sir George Macmillan has apparently been sent *Rewards of Wonder*. Of the seven books listed, only the latter can now be traced.

November The song *Lights Out* published in *The London Mercury*. 'Thoughts of New England', 'Smudgy Dawn' and 'Dawn' reprinted in J. C. Squire's *Second Selections from Modern Poets*.

December Writing new poems and song settings. Receives 'French books'.

1925

Sleep reprinted in *A Miscellany of Artistic Songs. I will go with my father a-ploughing* and *Carol of the Skiddaw Yowes* reprinted in *50 Modern English Songs*.

January Produces a large number of songs and poems, including a collectior for Annie Nelson Drummond called *To Hawthornden*.

February Writes *The book of Five makings* and 'corrects' the green manuscript notebook. Also writes four song settings.

March Writes seven song settings, including three of French poems, and many single poems. Also produces four new collections of verse: *Memories of Honour*, *Poems to the States*, *The Book of Lives and Accusations* and *Poems of Gloucester, Gloucesters and of Virginia*. Dr Robinson is replaced by Dr

	Randolph Davis, a Canadian with whom Gurney forms a rapport.
27 March	Arthur Benjamin performs two of Gurney's songs at a concert at Stone House.
April	Produces two new collections of poetry – *Six Poems of the North American States* and *Poems in Praise of Poets* – and many single poems. Also writes four song settings, including one to his own words called *Song of the Canadian Soldiers*. 'Schubert' published in *Music and Letters*.
May	Dr Davis is replaced by Dr Anderson.
June	Produces *Pictures and Memories* and many single poems. Also writes seven songs.
July	Writes five songs and one choral setting. Stainer & Bell publish *Sowing*.
August	Condition shows signs of slight improvement.
September	Writes eight song settings and some instrumental music.
November	Marion Scott and Ralph Vaughan Williams make plans to transfer Gurney to Dr Davis's care as a private patient.
December	Plans suddenly abandoned.

1926

	Revises a number of his earlier poems in a pink 'Student' exercise book. Stainer & Bell publish the song cycle *Lights Out*.
January	Dr Hart, a Harley Street psychiatrist, is consulted about Gurney's condition.
April	Taken by Marion Scott to see a play at the Old Vic and later writes a play called *The Tewkesbury Trial*. Completes *Best poems*. The song cycle *The Western Playland (and of sorrow)* published as part of the Carnegie Collection of British Music.
September	Produces many new poems but mental condition worsens.

November	Mental condition deteriorates further and he becomes agitated, stating that he 'should be allowed to die'. Refuses to be examined and asserts that an inspection of the floor and ceiling to find the machines torturing him would be more effective.
December	Becomes severely deluded and believes himself to be Shakespeare, Hilaire Belloc, Beethoven and Haydn, amongst others.

1927

	Stainer & Bell publish *Star Talk*.
February	Treated by Mr Lidderdale, a Christian Science practitioner, on the advice of Adeline Vaughan Williams.
March	Provided with a table to work on in the hospital gardens.
April	Mentally 'very confused' and treatment with Mr Lidderdale is terminated. 'Beethoven I wronged thee undernoting thus' published in *Music and Letters*.
May	Revises and 'corrects' poems by Walt Whitman.
June	Becomes hostile to hospital staff and fellow-patients. Physical condition deteriorates.

1928

	Oxford University Press publish *Walking Song*, *Desire in Spring*, *The Fields are Full*, *Severn Meadows*, and *The Twa Corbies*. 'To the Poet Before Battle' reprinted in Wallace Briggs's anthology *Great Poems of the English Language*. 'Song of Pain and Beauty' reprinted in H. R. L. Sheppard and H. P. Marshall's anthology *Fiery Grains*.
February	Victor Gollancz expresses interest in publishing a collection of Gurney's poems. Marion Scott

	assembles a selection and copies them out. Gurney's eyes are examined.

July   Miss Mollie Hart is paid 10s.9d for typing Marion
                      Scott's selection of Gurney's poems.

1929
4 March   Taken to Gravesend and Rochester by Marion
                      Scott. Wishes to buy a 'Phillips 1/- Atlas' but is
                      unable to find one and Miss Scott buys him an
                      edition of Shelley instead.
August   Claims to be the author of Shakespeare's plays.
28 Dec   Visits the Old Vic with Marion Scott to see an
                      afternoon performance of *A Midsummer Night's
                      Dream*.

1930

                      'Song of Pain and Beauty' and 'To the Poet Before
                      Battle' reprinted in Frederick Brereton's *An
                      Anthology of War Poems*. 'Song of Pain and Beauty'
                      also reprinted in W. H. Davies's anthology *Jewels
                      of Song*.

1931

                      'Tobacco' and 'Encounters' reprinted in *The
                      Mercury Book of Verse*.
June   Becomes 'very deluded & much persecuted by
                      wireless speakers'. He hoards rubbish and becomes
                      obsessed with 'underlining words in every book
                      which he picks up'. However, he 'continues to
                      write poetry'.

1932

                      Receives a number of visits from Helen Thomas,
                      the widow of Edward Thomas.
November   'Tobacco' and 'Encounters' reprinted in J. C.
                      Squire's anthology *Younger Poets of Today*.

1933

May   Physical and mental condition deteriorate further. Becomes 'very abusive and forceful'.

December   'Darkness has Cheating Swiftness', 'Old Thought', 'Old Dreams' and 'Towards Lillers' published in *The London Mercury*.

1934

January   'The Soaking', 'When March Blows', 'Robecq Again', 'Tea Table', 'Early Spring Dawn' and 'When the Body Might Free' published in *The London Mercury*.

May   'Defiance', 'Late May' and 'The High Hills have a Bitterness' published in *The London Mercury*.

August   Becomes apathetic and his memory begins to fail. Now believes that 'Collins the International' wrote Shakespeare's plays. 'Stars Sliding', 'Drachms and Scruples' and 'Possessions' published in *The London Mercury*.

1935

                   Gerald Finzi and Marion Scott make plans for the publication of a symposium on Gurney's work in *Music and Letters*. The possibility of publishing his songs is also discussed.

May   Receives treatment for his lumbago.

1937

February   Gerald Finzi and Marion Scott proceed with their plans for the publication of Gurney's work. The *Music and Letters* symposium begins to take shape.

April   Walter de la Mare agrees to write an introduction for an edition of Gurney's poems.

July   Becomes 'much weaker' physically and mentally.

23 November   Diagnosed as suffering from pleurisy and tuberculosis. Marion Scott is urged to visit because he is in 'very poor health'.

26 November   Sent proofs of the *Music and Letters* articles but is
                   too ill to open them.
26 December   Dies from bilateral pulmonary tuberculosis at 3.45
                   a.m.
31 December   Buried at Twigworth, Gloucestershire. Canon
                   Cheesman takes the service.

1938
January   Symposium on Gurney's life and work published
                   in *Music and Letters*. Oxford University Press
                   publish *Ivor Gurney: Twenty Songs* in two
                   volumes.

80 POEMS OR SO

The Change

The fields are bare now and the starlings gather,
Whirr above stubble and slow changing hedges;
Changed the season's chord too, now F major
Or minor. The gnats go plaining by the sedges.

And there is nothing proud now, not disconsolate;
Nothing youthful save where dark crocus flings
Summer's last challenge toward Winter's merciless
Cohort, for whom the robin alone sings.

The fields for a while longer, then, O soul,
A curtained room close shut against the rime –
Where shall float Music free, voice, and violin's
Denial passionate of the frozen time.

Western

A water clearness in the sparkling air
And shadows Summer-black on azure pools
December down-cast, January smiles,
And sees the ice thaw through without a care.

Before the dark come and Orion high
Swings his sign East to West, or Argo sail
To bourne beyond horizon, with true tale
Of how these meadows gloomed when he passed by.

But this land shows indeed the stars' true floor.
No man is dwelling in this lovely room
But strengths himself against his breathless doom
And lightless, with this dim wonder and frore.

Before Resurrection

The wind of March is out,
    Sense of daffodils
Through the quick blood thrills,
    Glories, hurries about.

The wind is royal yet,
    Far royaller
The memory of her
    That Winter's cruelty set
In frost-chains, she so eager,
    And the violet.

The blue and golden must
    Time endure somehow
Till March blow dust
    In Clouds, and the glow

Of the sun draw shadows
    Black-hard, strong;
And over meadows
    Skylarks throng.

Good Friday

Gray plumes of softest feathers
Are plainlands' clouds to-day.
Christ's Passion fills the worship
Of folk of reverency.

God's Sacrifice is valued
More high than God's rewards.
Gray Peter's Abbey towers
And worship Heaven towards.

Heaven's floor, the plain land's ceiling,
Past stretch of words is fine.
There is more here.... Here the True Temple
Of birds and man and kine.

First Spring

Now are there green flames springing by washed roads,
And colour where Winter black and gray thorn showed.
Shakespeare's a fashion with all lonely walkers,
And wonder with ruth mixes in the blood.

Miles and miles walk they, those schoolgirls and schoolboys
For daffodils and primroses with the lies
Of half a hundred trespasses upon them,
Who drown their sins with action and clear noise.

Dawn pales the stars a brief while earlier, day
By bright day and the stars take new array.
Only my dumbness mocks my search for speech,
Only the thing-accomplished makes delay.

Coming Dusk

Blue is the valley, blue that distant tower,
And Cotswold drapes in mist behind the azure;
In April has there come November's hour,
And there is melancholy without measure.

No apples dropping from trees, no chestnuts thudding,
Dumb Spring without a sign waits the day coming,
But in such drab trance nothing can come sudden;
Time hesitates, but moves to an East looming

With night gathering dusk banners of woe,
Shall out-front azure, and the gray road, winding:
A grizzen carpet folded very slow.
That valley soon will be hidden beyond finding.

Above Dryhill

Under the edge of Cotswold is a field,
Where one in Spring-time ploughs and finds a coin
Lost and lamented by some soldier's child
Or Roman private fifteen centuries gone:
And now potato leaf that field shows on –
The thronged ground-foliage – but the kite still hovers;
Trefoil, and cropped grass, height and steep slope covers;
And Spring as in Constantine's time is mild.
There the lean shepherd goes
And the flocks wander,
Lonely clouds and life
As lonely under;
And there the high wild hedges saw I tamed
And cunning woven when the green buds flamed
With deft inweaving like a player's showing
Of Bach's fourstranded thought,
Fixed pattern wrought
So easy and as cunning to move wonder.
In April's kindest and her softest day
I helped, as clumsy two-left-handed may,
Cutting the green briar from the horrid stem
And tangling every step in swathy thorn,
Curses as sharp as prickles from me at them
Sparked and jerked out. And still the easy blunder . . .

Spring Dawn

Smudgy dawn, scarfed with military colours,
Northward, and flowing wider like slow sea-water,
Woke in lilac and elm and almost among garden flowers.
Birds a multitude: increasing as it made lighter.
Nothing but I moved, by railings there. Slept sweeter
Than kings the country folk in thatch or slate shade.
Peace had the gray West, fleece clouds in its power.
Out on much-Severn I thought waves readied for laughter,
And the fireswinger promised behind elm-pillars
Showed of a day worthy of such dawn to come after.

Morning

In the white painted dark lobby,
The rosy fireshine is shown;
And the door keeps still its reticence
This morning, not yet broad grown.

And the mat is not moisted with fresh mud,
Since all above sleep on still:
I like that pale Winter-reflection
Gone truant from loving too well.

Spring's Token

The Cuckoo cry is Spring's
Most nearest token,
Strongest, by memory
Soonest awoken.

But of the colour-shimmer
On the withy bed,
And April's new-washed azure
What shall be said?

What of the cuckoo flower
And the celandine
That draws the heart, will not
Miss to be seen.

For the daffodil what man
Has found fit praise
Or shall, though he lie astare
Through rapt long days –

Pondering that alone;
His sense with gold
Lading, drenching till
More it could not hold.

And who for the violet
Has found a word
Fitting that sacredness
Save a bird? And that bird

Drunken with love-longing
Caught so far
Out of himself, he seems
Not a song, but a star.

Yet cuckoo's cry is Spring's
Most nearest token,
Strongest, by memory
Soonest awoken.

Rainy Midnight

Long shines the line of wet lamps dark in gleaming,
The trees so still felt yet as strength not used,
February chills April, the cattle are housed,
And night's grief from the higher things comes streaming.

The traffic is all gone, the elver-fishers gone
To string their lights 'long Severn like a wet Fair.
If it were fine the elvers would swim clear,
Clothes sodden, the out-of-work stay on.

April Gale

The wind frightens my dog, but I bathe in it,
Sound, rush, scent of the Spring fields.

My dog's hairs are blown like feathers askew,
My coat's a demon, torturing like life.

April Mist

Dampness clings about me as I walk
And the sun but filters through
High clouds unmoving, threatening rain.
Leaf mould clings, and the leafy drift below.

But how the green has sprung in a single night;
What sudden flood bears high the foam of May!
Pear trees and apple trees grown twice as bright
And pinpoints grown to buds between day and day!

Dull Afternoon

The sun for all his pride dims out and dies;
Afternoon sees not one
Of all those flames that lit the primrose lamps;
At Winter's hest; fordone.

Like music eager curving or narrowing
From here to there. Strange how no mist can dull
Wholly the silver edge of April song
Though the air's a blanket weighing on like wool.

Water Colours

The trembling water glimpsed thorough dark tangle
Of late-month April's delicatest thorn,
One moment put the cuckoo-flower to scorn
Where its head hangs by sedges, Severn bank-full.
But dark water has a hundred fires on it;
As the sky changes it changes and ranges thorough
Sky colours and thorn colours, and more would do,
Were not the blossom truth so quick on it.
And Beauty brief in action as first dew.

April 20 1919

There is no thread of all the day's colours
Has 'scaped my eyes. I have seen well to-day –
The deepest sweet taken of honey hours,
And bear to sleep fine memories away.

O may they haunt my dreams! Dear Sleep renew
Thirst and desire of sight in me, that is
Of all the threads of sense most nearest to
Godlike, and has the surest end of bliss.

Beauty that swells the bud, makes dense the grove,
Sets lambs leaping with tails twinkling and fills
The blackbird so with untoucht wonder of love,
He sings in the vale to awaken the echoing hills.

Sedges

I heard the white and brittle sedges make
A song of Autumn for the Spring come now,
And barred with wind-lines was their tiny lake
With dimpled notes of gray water in row:
But all their melancholy was nothing of use,
April's a girl, and Laughter her dearest use.

But, April, when you hand your garland over
To young May, shall not he give you scorn for scorn,
And if your hopes are to cheat him into lover
You'll rue that; he'll make you wish you had never been born.
Your faded buds he may take and make fun behind you,
The scorn of the sedges seek you out and find you.

Late September

The trees are breathing quietly to-day
Of coming Autumn and the Summer over;
Pause of high Summer when the year's at stay
And the wind's sick, that moves now like a lover.

On valley ridges where the beeches cluster,
Or changing ashes set by slopes of plough,
He goes; now sure of heart now in a fluster,
Of teasing purpose. Night shall find him grow

To dark strength and relentless-spoiling will.
First he loves baffle streams and dull the bright;
Cower and threaten both about the hill –
Before their death trees blast in full delight.

Moor and Ocean

There the gorse sea with yellow foam
Holds tracks to guide the sheep-boy home,
But here the vast and wandering floor
No set sign keeps for ever more.

Here in November mists great ice
Lurks, doom of tall ships, argosies,
The death of men; our moor desires
Strangers to shelter by bright fires.

Western Light

Our Western light has truths
Above all England's spaces,
Glories and tender ruths, unnumbered graces,
And winds of fruitfulness;
To poet not less
Than farm-hind or garden places.
Or slant orchards nobler none else than here.
A light of creation, a birth-light,
A day-being dear.
Endless gratitude
Of soft Atlantic breezes come
To some sort of home,
After a thousand miles no rood
Of Earth, no green, save heaving,
Silver none ever than foam.

The Bramble Patch

The flame so primrose pale
In sunset's glow
Rosy and golden is
And hot-heart now.

The sun has drawn with him
Light from the air:
Dusk breathes a lovely rest
After his glare.

With tender hands stars bless
The tired earth, let
A beauty misty fall
Of star-dew wet.

But the farmer not perceives,
His eyes ne'er raising
From the black and perished bramble
Or the still blazing.

He as they circles in
The path foremade
One with his work, a shade
In the bramble shade.

Cold Dusk

Now the red sun goes under
To a thousand foemen,
And dusk brings mystery
To all that Roman
Camp, height and common.

I am the trespasser
With thistles and waste things.
It is right to fear.
An owl cries warnings
From the dim copse near.

Bronze and Misted Moon

How did she swim into the sky
The bronze and misted moon;
Great Bear has lain him down on high
And dawn will touch him soon.
Pale not, bright sickle,
Till he grow fickle.

Till he grow tickle and break his chain,
Go hide in caves azure,
From whence with lower intelligence
He'll come at eve for sure.
Watch him, Heaven's darling;
Hark for his snarling.

Lovely Playthings

Dawn brings lovely playthings to the mind,
But sunset fights and goes down in battle blind.
The banners of dawn spread over in mystery,
But nightfall ends a boast and a pageantry.

After the halt of dawn comes the slow moving of
Time, till the sun's hidden rush and the day is admitted.
Sunset dies out in a smother of something like love,
With dew and the elm-hung stars and owl outcries half-witted.

London Dawn

Dawn comes up on London,
And night's undone,
Stars are routed
And street-lamps outed.
Great sodden clouds begin to sail again
Like all-night anchored galleons to the dawn,
From careful shallows to the outer main.
Lockhart's shows lively up Whitefriars Lane,
Sleepers beside river change their pain,
(Summer is better now the cloak's in pawn)
And the first careful coffee-stall's withdrawn.

Only the poet strolls about at ease,
Wondering what mortal thing his soul may please
And spitting at the drains, while Paul's as ever
Is mighty and a king of sky and river,
And cares no more, Much-Father, for this one
Poor child, although a poet-man and clever
Than any spit-kid of seven million.
He'll read a paper till the dawn is done.

Sights

Paul's looming huge above the Street of Fleet,
Paul's towering high above Cheapside, and Paul's
Seen everywhere from river, when March calls
Gusts from the quarters four to bellow and bleat,
And still most mighty clouds travel Heaven's Halls;
Or bookstalls where the hands are soiled so soon
With turning purchases doubtful often over.
Lover of which, O Muse, is the faithfullest lover
And justest of the town of Thames and Sea?

Nay, for these are of day, and crowds know such,
Busied with daily care, bemused over much
With gray ways and mean of common living.
Love is not earned so easy, and the giving
Of common recognisance is not taken
As level with his having who has seen shaken
Green leaves delicate against the faint stars.
Who Cleopatra her stone has marvelled at
So stable over dark waters of bright scars,
Or gone down doubtfully slippery steps,
Whereat the ebb tide laps
Has seen a water city past mooring piles
And barges in dark files
A Venice seen sudden as any film
Instantly wonderful, a water city,
A cloak-and-giltern river of Romance realm.
Thames flowing exquisite and witty
To sea and darkness from the lamps and calm.
These things to have seen are love's acceptance
And thousand things and one of merest chance.
London's bright jewels of indemnity
For miles of gray Hells, hours of hopeless ache.
She has her precious things
And keeps shrines secret yet for Beauty's sake.

The Road

Out beyond Aldgate is a road,
And a broad
Clean, noble thing it runs,
For the sun's
And wind's and man's delight,
And the high stars at night.
There go Jewesses
And Poles and Russ and these
Pale-faced sons,
Daughter of Thames and Paul's
Betwixt walls and high walls
Of sooted brick ugly turned.
A hard life, hardly earned;
Routine that galls,
Being to cunning turned.
Seldom marvellous
Comes dawn tremulous,
Or steady on that East
Is light increased
Through smoke-fog or river mist . . . .
Never fades the sun
Out in pageants that stun
The heart from talking thereon.
Always something mars
Magnificence from stars.
From strange faces and thunder
Men must draw wonder:
Thunder
Of trams and buses crammed,
Or Saturday-night dammed-
Up, seething, dodging,
Grumbling, laughing, over-busy
Crowd in Mile End crammed;

Or in one hour of joys
When football plays
Marvellous music on these jigging heart-strings,
And one lucky kick brings
Battle-winning in a Niagara of noise –
Or some furtive
Trick of professionalism
Plunges a crowd in Hell's
Own tumult and scorn and hot-alive
Furious cataclysm –
The referee quells.
Or in sight of a painted
Face, through the tainted
Smoke-blue atmosphere
Of Music-hall, Cinema,
Where happy Tom Parker
Or Chaplin would grin him a
Further defiance of consequence here,
Or in drinkings of beer,
Or eatings of strange fish
Or shelled things from barrows;
Stewed eels, winkles; –
Roast pea-nut mingles
Well with the whole.
Or in sight of fallen horses
Or axle-broken wheeled things
The market-gardener brings
Or the hawker, his cabbages,
Some Essex husbandryings
For London's vast maw.
Or fire-engine's law
Of free-way when the quickest sees
Smoke or sparks rising
In places surprising
And rings in fears' ecstasies,
For quick horseless carriages,

Brass-helmeted heroes –
But it might be advertising.
Anyhow folk live there
And daily strive there,
And earn their bread there,
Make friends, see red there
As high on the clean hills
Where soft sea-rapture fills
The gladdening lungs.
And young souls are fleshed there
And tyrant immeshed there
As in Athens or Ukraine.
And the heart hurts the brain
Or the spirit is lashed there,
And thought is as vain,
Hope constant, and smashed there,
As away a day's journey by train.

North Woolwich

Hellene memories barbed of the bright
Morning of new Time among tall derricks
And floating chimney-pots with empty tackle,

Drawn by fierce asp-things slowly out of sight;
For Sappho's easy happy mirth the cackle
Brittle that's not of help to odes or lyrics.

Houses like long Iliadian lines stretch on,
And railing shadows bar a recognisable
Of-no-man-questioned earth, whose chemistry

Of Marathon or Sparta kin must be.
The vault of air as stable
As on Olympus ringed with careless vines
Or where Ithaca seaward green inclines.

Speed is here, for bread is still to fetch:
And cunning, for milk spills from any vessel
The turnstile is through-gone without a wrestle.

But filled is every ditch,
No boys to show that smoothly running muscle.
Gaol waits for them would face without a stitch

Heaven's nakedness; those feet are black as pitch
Should gleam on gold sands white or in Stadium lines.
Can Aphrodite bless so evil dwelling,

Or Mercury have heed to Canning Town?
Nay, rather, for that ugly, that evil smelling
Township, One Christ from Heaven should come down,

Pitiful and comradely with tender signs,
And hot the tea, and shield a chap from fines,
A foreman carpenter not yet full grown.

Woolwich or So

There is a flat by Thames that floors the stars
So well that even Woolwich town not mars
The stillness and etched beauty of clear nights,
When hufflers go down stream with riding lights
Hung at the mast head, and the river's full
Of gliding, shifting, radiant shivers, beautiful
Of coloured lights and darks quicker than thought:
And there's a new spirit of the day-drear flats;
Romance hanging about the sooty slats;
Obscured or transfigured all that was dull,
Till dawn show white the starved and veering gull.

Western Sky-Look

When clouds shake out their sails
Before delighted gales,
I think the sailor-men at sea,
Hearing the engine throbbing free
Curse their today's fate that they must
Defeat Magellan with black dust,
Scrape deck-plates till the nerves are worn – ;
Whose fathers froze in desperate weather
Sail-handling in Death's despite together.
Here's never work that's fit for man,
Bristol Cabot, Drake, Magellan
Set man's strength set against the sea,
With courage broken and bulwarks lashed,
And seventh-Hell battle never drawn;
While here and now pale Duty does
Domestic service on bright brass . . . .
The sailor-men lift heart and eyes
To the thronged skies:
They cleave the air, leap winged to shake
More sails, more sails out; watch the wake
Of cirrus lengthen on the blue,
And run clean sailor-work to do . . . .
Fall sheer . . . to waste and paraffin –
Pistons gone tired of out-and-in,
Black work as hard and dull as sin.

Fine Rain

There's mirth in London streets,
Where the rain fleets
To silver every fur.
The lamps of Westminster
Haloed and laughing are,
Each peer of a star,
Each fine to the sight, and
Sure delight,
Misted and gorgeous each careering car.
Gentlemen with bowlers
And stand-up collars
Even, are amazed.
Aristocratic
Ladies ecstatic
For all their pride.
Children, O children, flit-armed, shiny-eyed . . .
But the old fellow by the orange barrow
So much has seen of wet or fine,
Of joy or sorrow,
From far West Hammersmith to Bethnal Green;
He bides and awaits morrow
With drab serene
Patience, bestows a sniff
On the half-noticed whole, and turns to barter
Oranges as if
London held nothing worthy of that sniff.

London Visitor

April walks the ways,
The heads of all
Are turned to watch her.
None to match her
For fairy grace,
And magical
Quick-thoughted face.

Through the whole gray city
She walks alone.
No courtiers near,
Scatters from her
With lovely pity
Beauty on men and stone;
A blue-sky bounty.

Charity untold, great-heart unrecking
Largesse of love.
That is her pleasure;
Light-bringer;
And, see her making
Silver above,
Cloud flocks, Heaven flecking!

In Town

The hills and valleys comforted
Men in distress when long-time-gone
The blessed Western air and sun
Magicked the whimsies in my head.

But here in London streets is naught
But gray discouragement, save how
The spirit of Man still keeps the glow
Drawn from his earth, from his air caught.

Yet one cloud rift in the upper air
Makes her that was a witch to seem
As some tale-princess waked from dream
Sleepy still, but drowsy-fair.

Home Thoughts

Soon the branches all will crowd with blossom, soon
Hedges be flooded with a foam of May
And the late wanderer under a sickle moon
The nightingale shall hear till first of day,
And I away, and my Love far away.

She walks where snow's eterne, I the uncomforting
Squares of that great city where Paul thrusts high
Huge sign of power, gulls float and squawk; cranes swing
Masses of steel like arms against the sky.

Why these I love, and she holds dear those hills,
But O for the small hedge-sheltered lanes and O
For daisy-fields and dancing daffodils,
Good lands where friends of mine, earth-tenders go
And Spring sets Earth aglow with tender thrills.

Town-Thoughts from Severn

O what does London look like now I wonder,
Russell Square, Kensington, Soho?
Are the March clouds up-piled like sighted thunder,
Onslow Square, delicate with cherry snow?

For Joy showers thick as apple-blossom on
All Severn-land; there is such happiness,
Largesse of peace from cloud and wind and sun
As never any Londoner might guess.

And yet I swear the costers and coal-heavers
Have courage, Will-to-Life as high as any
Dwellers by hills, valleys, or tiny rivers,
Be it Fretherne, Bredon Hill or Abergavenny!

On a Western City

I often think how strange those flowers are
To London town sold bright in so much drab:
Frail foreigners of peace amid the war
Of jostling business-people, rush of cab
And petrol-car, – a strained, unrested life,
Full of regrets, and reasonless swift strife.
But here the Island boys go out to gather
(A half-day travel) daffodils on red pastures;
Of hidden byways and lone copse are they masters,
And had rather
Start breakfastless under the first of day
Than tall daffodils let wither away;
Out toward Malvern now has April beauty
Scattered like crumbs to robins in the bare
Hedgerows and thin copses, and school boys there
Are decked with light beyond deserving's share.
Since in a thousand sooty towns of England
Young poets kill desire with thoughts of duty,
And study numb, drug soul with learning, they
Had rights to more than smoke stacks on the edge
Of heaven to watch, when poplars by the sedge
I have seen to-day: on scarred mounds, furze in bloom
And lady's-smocks prim – looked, for all that gay,
Yes, and tawn Bredon, sky's edge miles away,
With roads to Paradise everywhere leading,
Daffodils sprung like flames from red lands bleeding,
Timber and brick age old, and historied river
Blasted to furious gray tumultuousness
And racked down-sway.
In towns boys quarrel, whether they had liever
See Charlie Chaplin, Tarzan or the mess
Italian actors make of crockeries.
But here dispute runs of the earliest cuckoo,

Of eggs found cunningly, or the swimmer who
Should climb deep Severn further bank the soonest,
Or scale what highest tree for venturousness.
Paul's urchins spy the violets with surprise,
No wild flower, more this dim sprite blooms for them.
Daisies and wild things please their eager eyes,
And beauty is a sort of diadem
Worn on the drab breast of the russet town.
This Eastertide the London Churches will fill
With children who should seek the daffodil,
And anthems will mouths sing that dumb should be
Before the sudden store under the ringed tree.

On a Town

Rome, Florence, the bare names are spoken power
And this the Western City power in sight.
Who could be faithful to a dream delight
When realty holds so strong the actual hour?
Virgil's a name of awe, but must I dumb
Because the dead great praise another gloire?
Gloucester shall rich my lips and gild my store
Till Avalon return or high Sarras come,
And here an undercurrent of deep strength,
Still violent in rest, sure, quick on men
In casual day-business of fold or pen.
Mire takes on truth significant at length.
Disguise falls off from life so bright in show,
England, your garden is here, meaning, true glow.

Blessings

Michael, Peter, Paul, John
Bless the sunlight them shone on.
Nicholas and Maries too,
Bless while breath remains to do
Service. Crickley, Bredon, May,
Coopers, bless; but bless alway
The Abbey of Peter looking down
Imperial on Gloucester town.
All County Gloucester may God bless;
Hills, orchards, lanes no less
Than towns, hamlets, single homes –
Bless till crack of Doomsday comes.
Bless the Severn winding brown
From Tewkesbury to Bristol town.
Bless me, too, my foes, my friends . . . .
So this long tale of blessing ends.

Above Maisemore

O, lovely city! All the valley blue
Raiments thee like a garment of soft art,
The very home-thing of the tired heart,
Desire's own yearning, which to sorrow grew.
No marble nor gold mosque gleams out from thee;
Thy sober, usual beauty shows as one,
Yet drawn together by dominion
Of Peter's Abbey, ruling quietly.
Not loudest music is the sweetest, nor
The highest statua most noble seen.
Distant is azure over pasture green
And like the Promised Land your sight from far,
Sober and glorious, City of the Plain,
A thousand years stay so, and stay again.

The Town

The homely cities with plain Georgian look,
And small Elizabethan for the poor
Are good to be downnoted in a book,
Before progress has marched them out of door.
The alley ways and queer inconsequent
Marble, hoop, skipping playgrounds of the ragged –
Well to paint now, the County Council meant
To pull all John Smith Row down in a packet.
In these grave places, no broad way leads pompous
To Town Hall's looking like a pretty gaol.
No Drapery Emporiums like tomboys
Playing mad tricks to make an artist pale.
Here are the poor but dwelling out-of-country.
The rich not office people with a home;
Both love a horse, take pleasure in a tree.
Work ended, through the Tale of History come.
Here are mechanics still aware of earth
And masters have a love for marl and clay,
Both would wish land, labour, thought whose birth
Shall bear a harvest some far happy day.
And babies are not heavened by the Park
And girls are learned in flower names straight from Latin,
And dawn light and clear midnight, light and dark
Give one a guide of choice in wool or satin,
Where boys go leagues for flowers and know foxes' lairs,
Swim and get fish from out their border river,
And look a month off for September fairs,
And take football defeats like Judgement ever.
There the four ways, as Roman thought lay best,
Carry the country traffic to the mart
And a grave *Journal* mentorises best
A county glad of gossip for its part.
Elections are a neighbour man's affairs

And prosecution next street interest
A marriage, a child–birth, one's almost tears.
And certain sympathy Life's chiefest test.
The walking stranger first sees Abbey gray
Above fine trees, after a Middle-age
Town – outskirt without Villas, then must he say
'I have come home. This all men's heritage
Is': like a garment does the city wrap
His dusty tiredness, shade his torrid front,
Soothe soul with cool long drinks mayhap
Not shamed of Beer taken friendly, out of wont.
Where trams are rattly and a losing game
And 'England' is a thought of fields outside,
And Cricket, or strange journeys at Whitsuntide.

Time to Come

They will walk there, the sons of our great grandsons and
Will know no reason for the old love of the land.
There will be no tiny bent-browed houses in the
Twilight to watch, nor small shops of multi-miscellany.
The respectable and red-brick will rule all,
With green paint railings outside the front door wall;
And children will not play skip-games in the gutter,
Nor dust fly furious in hot valour of footer;
Queerness and untidiness will be smoothed out
As with any steam-roller tactful, and there'll be no doubt
About the dust-bins or the colour of curtains,
No talking at the doors, no ten o'clock flirtings,
And Nicholas will look as strange as any
Goddess ungarmented in that staid company,
With lovely attitude of fixéd grace,
But naked and embarrassed in the red brick place.

We see her well, and should have great thanksgiving,
Living in sight and form of more than common living.
She is a City still and the centuries drape her yet;
Something in the air or light cannot or will not forget
The past ages of her, and the toil which made her,
The courage of her, the army that made not afraid her,
And a shapely fulness of being drawn maybe from the air,
Crystal or mellow about her or above her ever:
Record of desire apparent of dreamer or striver;
And still the house between the Cotswolds bare
And the Welsh wars, Mistress of the widening river.

Alterations

Villas are set up where the sheep folds were
And plate glass impudent stares at the sun
For byres, and stack-boards. Threshing for ever done;
New things are there, shining new-fangled gear.

Peasants and willow pattern went together,
And whiskers with the white road suited well.
Now there's a mixtured hotch-potch hard to tell;
'Twill lame the mare, turn cream, and spoil the weather.

Change

Gone is the stubble
From the field I ploughed,
There bright potato leaves
Show in a crowd,
And the pewit calls no longer from under the cloud.

The short straw Roman
As armour seemed.
The moist soil parted
Sheered over and gleamed;
Gold lay in the furrows and field long streamed.

Grain is so noble;
The commoner thing
May have more virtue
Or more wealth bring,
But it is right to regret what poets may sing.

Near Redmarley

The shearing plough cuts red land
That ploughed when watchmen lit
Pile high on Malvern Beacon,
To tell Spain's fleet at hand;
Fired and stood off from it.

And hedges mend as ever,
There is no new craft there;
Whatever change at sea.
Gorse fires and scars show bare
No change, save Spain, whatever.

Brave Carpets

Brave carpets had the emperors of old,
Scarlet and gold inwoven, shaken fold on fold
On marble and syenite where their feet should fall
Going down graciously to embassies in High Hall,

Homage and body-splendour. But here in meadows
Kine and the errant conies move in shadows
And sleep on mantles emerald of costless stuff –
Where rain falls soft to renew and to assure enough.

There is a Valley

There is a valley soaked in with memories,
Cloister and Hearth, *The Prelude*, and Brahms' mellow –
A river loiters downward in rich ease,
To salmon and the Easter Bore's low bellow;
Meadows I think in plain land without fellow
And breathing lovely sense of song and books,
Charming half discord with its level looks;
Palm grows there, kingcups shall, and tansy yellow.

And these at last sun mild arts mix and wander;
Such tunes as twilight makes soft to the mind
No violent thing, but under labour wonder,
The sense and soul drowsed, leaving knowledge kind;
Fancy's patterns to wind and unwind,
Crochet-of-making, or a sort of tobacco taking
In afterglow, no steel to set the man on shaking –
Wisdom and Folly mixed in weaving blind.

A Farmer's House

In the white morning when the air kept still
A freshness and a cold from unsunned dawn,
A house said to me, 'I am Gloucester's will,
A thousand years' usage of mind and brawn,
Grown steady with the mark of centuries
And moving like a flood to common mean,
With gray soft spread curtains over blue sheen
And still with quiet of green spangled.
The clearness of the tiredness after labour
Borne me first in the mind of husbandman
Who for true love more than the rasp of neighbour,
In mind would build with roof of noble plan.
Not for respect a hovel against storm,
Not for ambition palace to gird friends:
But a child-bearing woman-knowing form
Who like a dog of honour, honours man.'
And now the house says, 'Look! Atlantic salted
And Severn softened air whose use delivered
Me and the meadow and hill sights.' The bolted
And gusty malice of Heaven has never shivered
One tree that shades the place, or loves the Spring here.
Content is full when Ashleworth bells ring here,
A type of England by the intellect
Not hindered and not faulted.

Valley Farm

Ages ago the waters covered here
And took the light of dayspring as a mirror:
Hundreds of tiny spikes and threads of light,
But now the spikes are hawthorn and the hedges
Are foamed like oceans' crests, and peace waits here
Deeper than middle South Sea, or the Fortunate
Or Fabled Islands. And blue wood-smoke rising
Foretells smooth weather and the airs of peace.
Even the woodchopper swinging bright
His lithe and noble weapon in the sun
Moves with such grace peace works an act through him;
Those echoes thud and leave a deeper peace.
If War should come here only then might one
Regret water receding, and earth left
To bear man's grain and use his mind of order,
Working to frame such squares and lights as these.

High Morning

The morning cloud has lifted
That veil of fleece so white.
The girl has left her milking,
And scours her metal bright.

Late afternoon she'll wander
Where blossom loves her youth,
But her true frame is morning
Of lucent lovely truth.

This County

By the Lord this county binds in most gracious things
And fancies miracles with contented breath!
Are there elsewhere such notes as her dawn-bird sings,
In the lilac there, or stray bushes beneath?

Dawn will strike that brave star soon, but not basely,
To fall past Malvern in a worthy slant.
Pale already are the failing valours that he
Fights and makes play with taunt thrown against taunt.

Dawn makes smooth the rough path of the day,
And satins clouds to life and prettiness.
Fall moon, hinder not you this soft sky-play:
What should an O do, but stare? – no more nor less.

Longney

These have grown grave-eyed by the smoothy river,
Who gleamed in glance and ran so hard and swift.
Life now has sobered them for ever and ever.

Though in the towns Life's known an evil gift,
And being but a bitterness thrust on,
Here is such sweetness in the wind's light lift.

And such a grace in action from the sun,
This folk is mild of heart; this folk had liever
Keep calm aside from crowds and hot endeavour.

Ashleworth

I would see the gray church spired again
And then die.
Other things are weariness; I am tired of them altogether.
There I am I.

And nothing but the river's mournfulness,
Or clouds wet to spoil
Attempts so feeble yet brave for happiness,
Cheating Time's guile.

The clouds' peace with the water peace there mixes,
Pasture's a third.
And one may read books there, Poetry fine flower,
Flame in the word.

The waggoners and bargemen and cowdrivers
I will get to know,
And talk to them, and draw peace and strength from them,
Live deep there and slow.

The Patroller

There was no sound within that golden room
But only the fire-mutter and still were we
Who watched fire palaces falling slow to doom,
And through and out in dreams to the troubled sea,

Where in the lash of rain and spray homelongings
The heart stabbed deep and keen, desiring so
Naught but in memory these weather wrongings
In such a silence, such a rosy glow.

Up on Cotswold

Men boast of stone walls stable here as hills,
But now the first springtide of whiteness fills
By-Severn with a flood not easily told,
Setting all one way Northward to the outer
And frozen seas not blessed of any bud.
They have not heard tansy or golden rod,
No flowers whatever,
Cotswold says 'See,
My hollows and my valleys are all spangled
With bright fires tiny.'
By-Severn would not have the question wrangled
But smiles by London sliding,
Scratch-faced serenely,
And looks her fill without sound or chiding.
O how settle the question between these
Neighbours and sisters jealous of their rank.
Shall's set the church bells clank?
By Bob Major or Minor decide degrees?
No, let us go by turns to either or other
And keep a silence, or a lying rather;
Day by day cheating each with friendly lies,
Those marvellous strange daughters of one mother.
Other folk for sin's sake must strain their souls
With lovely thoughts anxiously imagined;
Better live as I in a county where Beauty as bread
Is common and as dear.

Supposition

O were the Severn set to throw
Its waters over dyke and on
Those roads where great and poor have gone
To clash of metal, twang of bow,
So often long ago;
I could content me, leave the flooded
Meadow lanes, turn steady mooded
Where High Crickley fronts the day
A challenge and a threat alway:
Or where Cranham woods keep still
Fire of the Maker's Will;
To white Portway . . . .
But were these taken, the earth's crust
Rudely shaken, roughly thrust
By some dread force unmasterable
Crumbled to dust . . . .
Where should I turn, where look, that have
No life save Her's, that Gloucester gave
And shall give still.

Iliadian

Who laid blue Cotswold out so long in sun,
That far wall Iliadian; as over Troy
Smiled his content, so fair a beauty done.

A garden-land of gods, a noble play
A letting burn imagination
Beyond mere labour's bounds into a cry.

Beyond mere stuff to trumpet sound. Now March
Has drawn his train of white clouds Atlantic
Up Severn lined most featly under the arch.

And the mind fills with triumphs Homeric
Told us by Chapman in his numbers march,
That *Iliad* raised as golden brick by brick

Into a temple fit for Jove his own,
Mighty at birth, and yearly greater grown
And Cotswold sings that praise so greatly blown.

Personages

Beauty and bright fame go not together, I
Bought oranges to-day from Queen Deirdre.
Apollo hewed the beech, I stood and watched
A ghost of wonder weaving while one thatched;
A pattern of lithe movements all a wonder;
An axe one farmer dealt like Zeus his thunder,
But no harm came save splinters on the dog.
Rosalind milks brown Jerseys Brimscombe way,
With careless royal air born of the first breath
And stealthy air-stirrings of breaking day.
Young gods a many hew stubborn at their log,
Strong labours show the breed plain underneath,
And goddesses a many near.

Generations

There are runners yet on Cotswold,
Though Will Squele he lies low,
And men sow wheat on headlands
That other men see grow.

Eyes close and copper weights them;
Babes as blind come to birth;
Though John Gaunt's bets are ended
And shallow Shallow's mirth.

The Dursley School-Master

If he taught Dursley children, as 'tis said
And with vast patience earned a board and bed,
How must the Severn plain have entered in
His walking thoughts when school door was in pin.
Vast Egypt with her sandy spaces lay
Circont by Malvern and Wales up to the Hay,
And Nilus brought the elvers up on flood
(Framilode sent a many; they were good.)
Plain country talk all salted of the soil,
And Shallow, and young Hotspur (won the mile
In May Day races) Perdita, Viola; avoided;
With folk against one Coriolanus crowded
And all the clowns, with all the jests of men,
Feste, Touchstone, Bottom, Edgar, and Lancelot,
Their lucky phrases stuck, and not forgot,
The hardship brought the best of them to pen.
O dreams! O bright ambition, how was that?
Fulfil where Dursley Hill falls to the flat:
Was it not easier to trust for memories
In London town, with Court and stage to please.

April 23 1922

Now on this famed day, Shakespeare's day, I'd set
My mind to praise the clear line that has cheated
Often for me the lengths of road and late
Labour of making and the serious weighted
Tablets of wisdom dark upon the page,
From adverse or black-cored ill created.
Now on this day on high
South-west has ranged array
Of cloudy ranks by the wind's urge defeated
From his onsetting honourably retiring slow.
Blackthorn promises
On earth beside me,
A wealth of beauty
Soon, when May the swallow sees,
To run his sonnets in our thinking:
The fashion and close garb of Severn region,
Meadow and bright hedgerows beyond legion.
Now can no poet manage his own line,
Nor lover of the Muse take Author other,
The casual and curious both had rather,
The Stratford man than Athens', Florence', Rome's.
Out come the book-worms from their lairy tomes,
And live a space in sunlight of the day,
Conjectures and crabbedness general put away.
The pleased eye reading where the finger comes
Ariel's s song imagined with Bottom's bray,
The tree-sights and the coloured clays and loams
Of this good Western land depict lively.
In other lands the maker builds four square
And claps a roof on crafty as may be,
Most careful ordered from thought's first degree
And a world says 'A masterpiece is there',
But England sees a sight of wind and storm,

A tournament, or crowd with passion swayed,
A man of learning, or of skilful blade
Seizes, wrestles, fights, has it into form:
Life lively mocked as ever maker made,
Outdoing what more stricter folk perform,
And sweet the picture as the Severn glade.
We are lovers all now of simplicity,
Of bright or bitter truth in naked sound,
A celebration of familiar ground;
Some praise of England or her circling seas
Or maiden in her ruthful passion drowned.

'Now are the hills born new in sparkling light'

Now are the hills born new in sparkling light
And all things take on movement once again.
Night with those high stars goes from thought of men
And one great flame is set for man's delight.
The ploughmen and milk maidens are gone out
To comradeship with kine of steaming breath.
They draw the air of morning's youthful faith
Before fire sets the dew-drops all to rout.

Shakespeare's Day

In one short six hours I saw Malvern stream
A mane of black smoke but no burn-gorse gleam
Royal that was; and meadows ready never
More, nor the hawthorn-brake, for Bottom, Weaver;
Malvern and Cotswold, Hereford, Clee and Wales
Roads noble, swept by wet and odorous half gales
And over all familiar as marching friends
Great rocky clouds in coloured lines without ends
And farm-folk lifted straight out of his pages
(Act one, Scene two) no pomp, no pet-rages;
All natural and free-given as water, free
To any walking thing as Charity
When actors famed play scenes for dogs forlorn.
The property was worth my while alone,
Actors were part perfect and April played
Scene shifter to a wonder for a maid
Only, the parts played dumb, I was made spout
Perdita and Titania to the heath out.
None were to hear but April and the cows
Nor wonder at my bent or smiling brows
Small pay, but for Garrick himself a right house.

April 23 1922

What fame is hers,
This England in the strengths Atlantic bound?
What honour most inhabits of her ground?
What, free of fears
Goes current with her name, who hears the sound
'England'?
Sure, that one Warwick style of youth that had
Misfortune with the Justice in some mad
Deer-stalking freak, and held horses they say;
Played ghost and Adam in a luckier day.
Got money, bought a house and farm or two,
Died. Leaving poets else not much to do.
Save praise an *Alchemist* or *Iliad*.
What eventuality! What a crew!

May Day

Chambers and tiring-rooms
For *'Summer-night's Dream* there.
Meadows of tall-wall trees
White-thorn and willow glooms.
These green-lit robing chambers
For careful wearing fitted –
May finds them cleanly quitted,
Save for an unthought number
Of small delicate swift
Trinkets of April fancy.
As mote-beams are they dancy,
And swing in light winds' lift.
All's ready; prompters save.
There's here too much good-nature
Since Nature is the teacher
And Shakespeare's play we'll have,
Bottom shall prompt Puck,
Peasblossom, Snug the joiner,
Starveling, Titania;
And laughter with good luck
Shall guard our company through.
But be you not regarding,
The bronzed and rough carving
That's floor beneath high blue;
See you rant not that glory
Your quiet lines in telling.
It makes curious fantasy
But spoils your mystery.
See the poplar impatient
Trembles, the cuckoo flower
Has been ashen this hour –
Begin! – uncivil, insatient.

Roads

Roads that lead like king's highway of ceremony,
Unrolling like a ribbon before one's thought,
A passage between hedges, or ancient right-of-way,
Lovely and worthy symbols, greatly fraught,
With high, false sights of fluttering pennonry
And fancied sounds of armour and war tool –
Echoes of strife in coloured ancientry
When king and baron each set each to school.
O but a poem's thought it runs so slow
When Malvern's picture full fills fantasy,
And Foscombe Hill already is aglow
This early April with gorse decoratory
And Severn's a gray sea of narrow bounding,
And Bredon smites imagination to confounding,
And *Summer Night's Dream* is the level flow
Of common thinking, casual poetry....
So gracious the rich store travellers aye surrounding,
And white and broad ways lead the feet thereto
That might on stubborn pavement walking be.
The eyes for Cotswold Kingsway have for rounding
O incredible rich packed stores of sight there shows
Where Corse road to Wainlodes breaks West and goes
Severn traversing ominous with threatening glee.

Walking Song

The miles go sliding by
Under my steady feet,
That mark a leisurely
And still unbroken beat,
Through coppices that hear
Awhile, then lie as still
As though no traveller
Ever had climbed their hill.

My comrades are the small
Or dumb or singing birds,
Squirrels, field-things all
And placid drowsing herds.
Companions that I must
Greet for a while, then leave
Scattering the forward dust
From dawn to late of eve.

Bridges

There are good arches in this land of ours,
Under Cotswold lying or away in the plain,
By Frampton there, or Maisemore's stately way,
You may stop the hundredth time to scan them again.

Or by Upleadon where the mill-fall goes,
Or Framilode where furious runs that race;
Over's long Bridgeway swift and white to see,
Whose builder ended there in false disgrace.

Or that small roadway arch where the Bore broke
Thundering a sudden up the brook, and made
A strange spray by the stray elms at Minsterworth
A gunnoise made me startle even half afraid.

The bridge high above Leadon near Redmarley,
A tiny Longford thing, and Stroud-way bridges;
Cranham's clear-streamed arch, and the brickbat things
Some good, that take the farmer over his ditches.

But up on Cotswold: Burford, Bourton, Swells
The loveliest of water arches have.
I boast about my country while 'tis wise
But those white trackways, O but they are brave!

The Companions

On uplands bleak and bare to wind
Beneath a maze of stars I strode;
Phantoms of Fear haunted the road
Dogging my footsteps close behind.

Till Heaven blew clear of cloud, showed each
Most tiny baby-star as fine
As any jewel of kings. Orion
Triumphed through bare tracery of beech.

So unafraid I journeyed on
Past dusky rut and pool alight
With Heaven's chief wonder of night
Jupiter, close companion.

And in no mood of pride, courteous
Light-hearted, as with a king's friend,
He went with me to the journey's end,
His courtiers Mars and Regulus.

My door reached, gladly had I paid
With stammered thanks his courtesy
And theirs, but ne'er a star could see
Of all Heaven's ordered cavalcade.
The inky pools naught held but shade,
Fine snow drove West and blinded me.

Midnight

There is no sound within the cottage now,
But my pen and the sound of long rain
Heavy and musical, I must think again
To find so sweet a noise, and cannot anyhow.

The soothingness and deep-toned tinkle, soft
Happenings of night, in pain there's nothing better,
Save tobacco, or long most looked for letter . . . . .
The different roof-sounds. House, shed, loft and scullery.

Quiet Fireshine

Quiet is fireshine when the light is gone;
The kettle's steam is comfort and the song
Now all the day's business stills down and is done,
To watch them seems but right; nothing at all is wrong.

Save the dark thoughts within most bitter with
The acid of betrayal, weak and black.
Regret for lost youth, loathe of useless strife
And peace of heart too difficult to get back.

Quiet is fireshine, and the mind would soak
Years ago, after football, in rich light.
Now the slack body and soul after the yoke
Are stale, too spent for dreams at fall of night.

Fragment

I think the taste of Realty is such
As waters of Dead seas long left lost inland
That no Heaven's mercy sweeten can by much,
Rasping the tender touch of any hand,
Blinding the eyes.
When the bright day that should arouse such joys
Is cover but for griefs of roughest kind
And lies stronger than Truth make truthful noise
Before the black night let the tired eyes blind.
Flesh is so strong, demands the spirits whole;
There is no surplus for the dying fire;
Realty has never margin for desire,
And matter's the true business of the soul.
Why breath should be blown so into coward stuff
Is yet obscure, there will no law obey
But its own stray
Inclining.
A wandering troublesome vapour out of restraining.

I Love Chrysanthemums

I love chrysanthemums and Winter jasmin
Clustering lichened walls a century old,
Ivied windows that the sun peeps in
When dawn an hour gone sees his level gold,
But for my Love, Sweet William, snowdrops, pansies,
Else she is cold.

And all the host of tiny or mighty things
Scattered by April, daring Autumn frost,
Or of man's hand, scarcely her imaginings
Touch, being save to these three, careless almost
And save to me. This knowing, should I envy
Princes of proudest cost?

The Garden

The ordered curly and plain cabbages
Are all set out like school-children in rows;
In six short weeks these shall no longer please,
For with that ink-proud lady the rose, pleasure goes.

I cannot think what moved the poet men
So to write panegyrics of that foolish
Simpleton – while wild-rose as fresh again
Lives, and the drowsed cabbages keep soil coolish.

Common Things

The dearness of common things –
Beech wood, tea, plate-shelves,
And the whole family of crockery –
Wood-axes, blades, helves.

Ivory milk, earth's coffee,
The white face of books
And the touch, smell, feel of paper –
Latin's lovely looks.

Earth fine to handle;
The touch of clouds,
When the imagining arm leaps out to caress
Gray worsted or wool clouds.

Wool, rope, cloth, old pipes
Gone warped in service;
And the one herb of tobacco,
The herb of grace, the censer weed,
Of whorled, blue, finger-traced curves.

Apprentices

We who praise poets with our labouring pen
And justify ourselves with laud of men
Have not the right to call our own our own,
Being but the ground-sprouts from those great trees grown.
The crafted art, the smooth curve, and surety
Come not of nature till the apprentice free
Of trouble with his tools, and cobwebbed cuts,
Spies out a path his own and casts his plots.
Then, looking back on four-square edifices
And wind-and-weather standing tall houses
He stakes a court and tries his unpaid hand;
Begins a life whose salt is arid sand;
Of cactus whose bread comes, whose wine is clear,
Being bitter water from fount all too near.
Happy if after toil he grow to worth
And praise of complete men of earlier birth
Of happier pen and more steel-propertied
Nerves of the capable and the mighty dead.

Doom's Tongues

On windy nights Doom's tongues sound very strange;
Sounds butting into dark tides broad of gloom.
There's guard from strangeness in warm lighted room,
Time smoothlier goes than is meant by change.

And there's a tale of hunted things gone quick
Unpathed to Bredon – but warm fire's thoughts drive
Fear to dark corners; Books are of all alive,
Most in the glow-flood, slow and deep and thick.

Compensations

Spring larch should set the body shaking
In masterless pleasure,
But virtue lies in a square making –
The making pleasure.
True, the poet's true place is in that high wood,
And his gaze on it,
But work has a bent, and some gray sort of good.
Worship, or a sonnet?

The Crocus Ring

O show to me a crocus ring
That dances round a bush of green
And I will make a lovely thing
To match the magic seen.

And swift the words should run to place,
Their rhyming fall inevitable,
The crocus come to show its face
In sound set well.

Children should read with bright eyed wonder
And long to dance as flowers do
Or Fairies, in and out and under
Brambles and dew,

Clap hands and call for country-going,
But O how false does memory
Play with a golden circlet growing
Round a March tree!

Polite Request

River mists and tall reeds
    Make me a song
That escaped my hurrying mood
    And drive along.

Straining limbs cannot
    Leave enough ware
The mind, or the thing that loves
    Making four-square.

A lovely dancing mix
    Of reeds and water. . . .
Too hard for me is truth
    In rhyming matter.

The Ship

A ship of silver sailed among
Cloudlets and stars: I saw her ride
On Night's blue tide,
Her freightage song.
A silver music packed her hold,
High argent glories manifold.

And poor men rapt in alleys vile,
With upturned faces, felt the stir,
Wind-beat of a messenger
Trouble the air,
Numbing awhile
Pain and the dull-aching monotony
With loveliest compassion, Divine pity.

The Square Thing

At Norton Green the tower stands well off road
And is a squareness meaning many things;
Nearest to us, the makers had abode
Beside the Northern road of priests and kings.

Men of a morning looked away to Wales
Or wavy Malvern under smoothy roof;
And said, 'That we have seen such hills and vales
Our churchkin here must give men certain proof.'

And so from virtue mixed of sky and land
They raised a thing to match our equal dreams.
It was no common infire moved their hand,
Building so squarely among meadow streams.

Daily

If one's heart is broken twenty times a day,
What easier thing than to fling the bits away,
But still one gathers fragments, and looks for wire,
Or patches it up like some old bicycle tire.

Bicycle tires fare hardly on roads, but the heart
Has an easier time than rubber, they sheathe a cart
With iron, so lumbering and slow my mind must be made,
To bother the heart and to teach things and learn it its trade.

The Cure

If aches were cured in rueing
Then grumbling would be well,
Or gates light in undoing
Worth while to scheme in Hell.

But since the run of fortune
Is hard and all too strait,
I'll make my way to Mortune
For dreams of faded date.

Depression

Misery weighed by drachms and scruples
Is but scrawl on a vain page.
To cruel masters are we pupils
And escape comes careless with Old Age.

O why were stars so set in Heaven,
To desire greedily as gluttons do,
Or children trinkets – May death make even
So rough and evil as we go through.

Moments

I think the loathed minutes one by one
That tear and then go past are little worth
But nearer to the blindness to the sun
They bring me, and the farewell to all earth.

Save to that six foot length I must lie in,
Sodden with mud, and not to grieve again
Because the Autumn goes beyond my pen
And snow for me is all too pure of stain.

Generations

The ploughed field and the fallow field
They sang a prudent song to me.
We bide all year and take our yield
Or barrenness as case may be.

What time or tide may bring to pass
Is nothing of our reckoning.
Power was before our making was
That had in brooding thought its spring.

We bide our fate as best betides,
What ends the tale may prove the first.
Stars know as truly of their guides
As we the truth of best or worst.

Introduction to Notes

The notes to the poems have the following structure: the page reference and title are followed by a brief history of the source, development and publication of the poem. We use the symbol • to note when the poem is here published for the first time. We then list the manuscripts and typescripts of the poem in a conjectural chronological order, including the copy-text we use indicated by bold type. We then list the first publication and major publications where the poem has appeared in print (those who wish to follow where poems have appeared in anthologies can do so in *Ivor Gurney: Towards a Bibliography*). Following this we give any information on text or title, and then gloss or comment on words or detail that may not be obvious to those not steeped in Gurney's ways. We have not annotated all the geographical locations, but we have provided a map of Gurney's Gloucester and Cotswolds to locate the places he mentions.

We give below a list of the manuscripts used and the abbreviations by which we refer to them. We have not listed all the typed or manuscript *copies* of versions of the poems which were subsequently done by Marion Scott, Joy Finzi, John Haines and so on, when these were mere copies produced with no input from Gurney himself. Readers should be aware that editors have used different versions of many of the poems, and we have re-edited all the poems from the sources indicated. We also list below the major published texts and the abbreviations we are using for them; other individual publications will be mentioned in the notes.

We use a two-part citation for the manuscripts and typescripts to give two different sorts of information. The first element of the citation represents the group of papers from which the individual document originally comes and the second represents the present location in the Gurney Archive in Gloucester. It is essential to use this two-part system because the actual documents have been used for a variety of purposes and ordered and re-ordered according to different principles, and the original relationship of some groups has been obscured by their wide dispersal in the archive. We have used abbreviations which indicate the nature of the document or refer to some distinctive feature of the paper used. Carbon copies are indicated by an asterisk. A single manuscript not part of a group will be noted under the individual poem as IM (for Individual Manuscript) and its number in the Gurney Archive.

Sources and printings
Texts which feed into 80 Poems or So:

GPB:	Small green pocket book, used by Gurney during his visit to Cornwall at Christmas 1918 and subsequently. Contains fragments and ideas for poems.
SS:	Small sheets of lined paper torn from a pad and numbered 1 to 7. Possibly the 'set of verses in rough' mentioned by Gurney in January 1919.
1LS:	Long sheets of lined paper, undated but in use at the same time as SS above. Contains early versions of poems in RMS below.
RMS:	Red 'Ayliffe' brand hard-cover manuscript notebook, in use by June 1919.
Howells	Howells papers, now in the Gurney Archive. See R. K. R. Thornton, 'New Howells–Gurney Papers', *The Ivor Gurney Society Journal*, 1 (1995), 69–76.
1EB:	Pages torn from missing exercise book; undated; one of the sources for Dorothy Gurney's typescripts.
2LS:	Long sheets of lined paper; undated; another source for Dorothy Gurney's typescripts.
3LS:	Long sheets of lined paper; addition of A or B indicates selection for typing. Undated, but another source for Dorothy Gurney's typescripts.
DG:	Dorothy Gurney typescripts, on thin paper, some with 'Bar-Lock' watermark; contain revisions in black ink by Ivor Gurney. This was the material submitted to Sidgwick and Jackson in May 1922, and forms the basis of this edition.

Texts which develop poems in this collection:

4LS: Long sheets of lined paper, undated but probably late 1921 or early 1922; 3 fair-copy poems.

BMS: Black hard-cover manuscript notebook, undated, but the address at '1 Westfield Terrace, Longford, Gloucester' suggests 1921–1922.

GMS: Green hard-cover manuscript notebook; title page bears inscription: 'the Note book (between music makings) of Ivor Gurney 1921–1922 <u>corrected</u>. <u>Feb 1925.</u>'

PMS: Pink marbled hard-cover manuscript notebook, undated but containing poem dated April 1922.

PTS: Set of typescripts on horizontal-line wiremark paper, transcribing PMS, but with Gurney's manuscript corrections of May 1923.

HAW: Typescript set *To Hawthornden*, assembled by Gurney in January 1925.

STU: Pink 'Student' brand exercise book, containing poems dated February 1926.

RVW: Typescript set on 'Royal Charter Bond' produced in 1943 at the instigation of Ralph Vaughan Williams. Contains all that remains of the final version of *Rewards of Wonder*.

Published versions

Blunden *Poems by Ivor Gurney*, Principally Selected from Unpublished Manuscripts with a Memoir by Edmund Blunden (Hutchinson, 1954).

Clark *Poems of Ivor Gurney 1890–1937*, with an Introduction by Edmund Blunden and a Bibliographical Note by Leonard Clark (Chatto & Windus, 1973).

Grigson Geoffrey Grigson, 'Six Poems by Ivor Gurney', *The Times Literary Supplement*, no. 3993 (13 October 1978), p.1136.

Kavanagh *Collected Poems of Ivor Gurney*, Chosen, Edited and

with an Introduction by P. J. Kavanagh (Oxford
University Press, 1982).

Palmer   Christopher Palmer, *Herbert Howells: A Centenary Celebration* (Thames, 1992).

PN Review 101   George Walter, 'Unpublished Poems by Ivor Gurney 1: "The best of the young men below the horizon"', *PN Review*, vol. 21, no. 3 (January/February 1995), pp.22–6.

PN Review 102   George Walter, 'Unpublished Poems by Ivor Gurney 2: "An unsuccessful and angry poet"', *PN Review*, vol. 21, no. 4 (March/April 1995), pp.25–9.

Walter   *Everyman's Poetry: Ivor Gurney*, selected and edited by George Walter (Everyman, 1996).

Notes on the Poems

The Change (p.39) **3LS 64.12.8**; BMS 64.4.3; Grigson; Kavanagh, 99; Walter,16.

Western (p.40) • **3LS 64.12.26**. The Miltonic/poetic 'frore' in the last line means 'intensely cold' or 'frosty'.

Before Resurrection (p.41) • GPB 2; 1LS 53.39–40; RMS 67.12–12v; **DG 64.11.18**; DG 12.3.14*; BMS 64.4.10–10v. Also called 'March'. Dated 'Gloucester Feb. or March 1919' on Marion Scott's manuscript IM 42.3.114–15.

Good Friday (p.42) • **DG 21A.152**. Gurney emphasises tradition by reminding us that Gloucester Cathedral was built on the site of St Peter's Abbey and by using 'kine', an archaic plural of 'cow'.

First Spring (p.43) **DG 19.123***; DG 64.11.14; Humanities Research Centre, University of Texas, Austin (*Letters*, 538). His letter to Blunden sends him a copy of the poem with the comment, 'Here is one of mine, which I like.'

Coming Dusk (p.44) **DG 19.122***; DG 64.11.12; *PN Review 102*, 27–8. Gurney has insisted on keeping his word 'grizzen', presumably meaning 'grey', though it is not in the *OED*.

Above Dryhill (p.45) • 2LS 21A.168; **DG 19.132***; DG 64.11.19. Title amended from 'Edge'; DG 64.11.19 has manuscript title 'Under an Edge'. Constantine the Great, the first Roman emperor to adopt Christianity, was emperor in the West from 312 to 324 and sole emperor from 324 to 337.

Spring Dawn (p.46) 1EB 70.34; **DG 64.11.24***; GMS 64.3.10; *The London*

Mercury, vol. IX, no. 51 (January 1924), p.235; *Second Selections from Modern Poets* (London: Secker, 1924), 221; Blunden, 84; Clark, 58; Kavanagh, 143; Walter, 49. Also called 'Smudgy Dawn'. Its appearance in *The London Mercury* conflated with 'Dawn Came Not Surprising' (the version which Clark prints) and the separation into two poems in *Second Selections from Modern Poets* stirred Gurney into substantial rewriting of this poem in November 1924 (IM 44.113).

Morning (p.47) **3LS 64.12.14**; IM 44.34; HAW 42.10.9; Clark, 47; Kavanagh, 94. Also called 'The Awakening' or 'First Morning'.

Spring's Token (p.48) • 1LS 53.35 + 52.11.168 (one text); **3LS 64.12.27–28**. Rejected by *The Spectator* in August 1919.

Rainy Midnight (p.49) **DG 64.11.21***; Grigson; Kavanagh, 101; Walter, 22. Fishing for the young eels called elvers – considered a delicacy in Gloucestershire – was a night-time occupation carried out with lamps and was popular on the Severn.

April Gale (p.50) **DG 21A.164**; Kavanagh, 91; Walter, 23.

April Mist (p.51) • **DG 19.39**; DG 12.3.3*; BMS 64.4.16. Also called 'April Morning'.

Dull Afternoon (p.52) **DG 19.37**; DG 21A.163*; BMS 64.4.15v; Kavanagh, 92. Also called 'April' and 'April – Dull Afternoon'.

Water Colours (p.53) **3LS 64.12.5**; Blunden, 31; Clark, 46; Kavanagh, 96. Gurney uses the archaic disyllabic form of the preposition 'through' in lines 1 and 6.

April 20 1919 (p.54) ILS 52.11.168; Howells; *The Royal College of Music Magazine*, vol. XVI, no. 3 (Midsummer Term 1920), 9; **DG 19.46**; BMS 64.4.18v; Palmer, 451; *PN Review 101*, 24. Also called 'I Have Seen Well Today'. The second stanza has been heavily amended on the copy-text from:

> O may they haunt my dreams! Dear Sleep renew
>
> Banners of high Spring that at the first
>
> Of dawn I may awake, Joy pulsing through
>
> To slake at Beauty's fount so bright a thirst.

Sedges (p.55) • **DG 19.124***; DG 64.11.13.

Late September (p.56) 2LS 64.12.12; **DG 18.43a**; DG 60.6*; BMS 64.4.2v; Grigson; Kavanagh, 96. Also called 'Quiet Talk' and 'The Trees are breathing'. Dated 'September 1920' on 2LS 64.12.12. The variant of 'will' for 'loves' in line 10 makes the meaning clearer.

Moor and Ocean (p.57) SS 53.43; RMS 67.15v; **DG 21A.166**; BMS 64.4.11, STU64.10.5; *PN Review 101*, 24. Rejected by *Harper's Magazine* in 1919. Gurney wrote to Marion Scott that 'Alas, you are right about "Moor and Ocean"! I must try again, for there is stuff therein' (*Letters*, 483).

Western Light (p.58) • **3LS 64.12.22**; 19.116; 42.3.77.

The Bramble Patch (p.59) • RMS 67.5; IM 42.4.5; IM 83.14.1-3 (*Letters*, 486); **DG 21A.161***; DG 64.11.16. IM 42.4.5 is dated 'Crickley Hill May 1919'. It is the last stanza that causes Gurney most difficulty and the version in this letter makes it a little clearer: 'He as the stars does keep / The path foremade . . . ' The poem called 'The Bramble Patch' at STU 64.10.12v–13 is a distant derivative of this poem.

Cold Dusk (p.60) • **DG 19.131***; DG 60.2.

Bronze and Misted Moon (p.61) • **DG 19.130***; DG 60.3. The Great Bear, *Ursa Major*, is a large constellation in the Northern sky.

Lovely Playthings (p.62) 1EB 64.12.1; 1EB 64.12.2; **DG 64.12.3***; 4LS 64.12.2; GMS 64.3.17v; Blunden, 81; Kavanagh, 144; Walter, 22.

London Dawn (p.63) IM 70.27-28; IM 70.25-26; **3LS 64.12.18**; BMS 64.4.5v-6; IM 55.34-35; IM 15.146; IM 44.10-12; Hurd, 137; Kavanagh, 61; Walter, 17. Also called 'Dawn on London'. A version of this poem was sent to the editor of *The Outlook* in 1921 or 1922 (*Letters*, 513.) Gurney's London poems are dominated by St Paul's Cathedral, and centre on an area around Whitefriars. Lockhart's, a chain of hotels and refreshment rooms, had a branch in Whitefriars Street.

Sights (p.64) 1EB 64.12.19-20; **DG 21.17A***; *The London Mercury*, vol. VII, no. 39 (January 1923), 241; *PN Review 102*, 27. As he does with Gloucester, Gurney focuses on the Cathedral (here St Paul's) and then looks at the area around it: Fleet Street, Cheapside and Cleopatra's Needle, an obelisk set up on the Victoria embankment in 1878. Gurney's 'giltern' is an idiosyncratic version of 'gilden' or 'golden'.

The Road (p.65) 2LS 82.38-40; **DG 19.54-55***; BMS 64.4.22v-24; *The Spectator*, vol. 130, no. 4787 (31 March 1923), 551; Walter, 24–6. Also called 'Beyond Aldgate'. Aldgate leads out to Whitechapel, Mile End Road, Commercial Road and the docks that Gurney describes in 'North Woolwich'. Gurney refers to the downfall of tyrannies in ancient Athens and modern Ukraine, which suffered tyranny and revolutionary upheaval throughout this period of Gurney's writing.

North Woolwich (p.68) **3LS 64.12.15-16**; BMS 64.4.21v–22; Blunden, 24; Kavanagh, 58. Gurney's picture of North Woolwich and neighbouring Canning Town slums is pricked by memories of ancient Greece. He encounters noise that is not as conducive to poetry as that round Sappho, the Greek lyric poetess of the 7th century BC. He compares the long lines of terraced houses to the fourteen-syllable lines of Chapman's translation of Homer's *Iliad*. He finds Woolwich, with its naval dockyard and barracks, kin to

Marathon and Sparta, which are closely associated with war; and the air seems to be as calm as that round Olympus, the home of the Gods, or Ithaca, Odysseus' Ionian island. He concludes that Christ is more appropriate to English needs than the Greek goddess of love and beauty, Aphrodite, or the Roman god Mercury, the tutelary deity of thieves and tricksters as well as god of science, eloquence and the arts.

Woolwich or So (p.69) **DG 19.133***; DG 60.1; *PN Review 102*, 28. Woolwich is an area where the dockyards and barracks provide an industrial scene not to Gurney's taste. 'Hufflers' are Thames barges. Evidently in response to a query, Gurney has written below the poem: 'riding lights are mast head lights, surely?' Riding lights are special lights displayed when a ship is riding at anchor.

Western Sky-Look (p.70) **3LS 64.12.20–21**; *The Nation and Athenaeum*, vol. 29, no. 21 (20 August 1921), 738; Walter, 15. Ferdinand Magellan (c.1480–1521), John Cabot (*c*.1455–*c*.1499), who sailed from Bristol, and Sir Francis Drake (1540–1596) are the great navigators.

Fine Rain (p.71) SS 53.41–42; RMS 67.16; *The Nation*, vol. 28, no. 20 (12 February 1921), p. 664; **DG 19.29**; DG 12.3.16*; BMS 64.4.11v–12. Also called 'Drizzle'. Marion Scott's transcript and typescript at 42.3.99–102 are dated 'February 1919'. The obscure 'flit-armed' (which Gurney writes in twice to show he means it) replaces 'gesturing' and means something like 'nimble-gestured'. Westminster, West Hammersmith and Bethnal Green are London districts.

London Visitor (p.72) • GPB 2; RMS 67.10–10v; **DG 19.26**; BMS 64.4.9v. Rejected by *The Spectator* in August 1919.

In Town (p.73) GPB 2; 1LS 53.28–28v; RMS 67.8–8v; **DG 82.35**; *PN Review 101*, 25. In a letter of April 1919 to Marion Scott, thanking her for her 'long criticism of my poems', Gurney says that 'I fancy "drab" must take the place of "witch", that's all' (*Letters*, 483). Rejected by *The New Witness* in August 1919.

Home Thoughts (p.74) 1LS 53.29; RMS 67.10v–11; **DG 82.30***; *PN Review 101*, 25. Also called 'Forethoughts'. Dated 'Hammersmith Feb 1919' on 1LS 53.29. Rejected by *The New Witness* in August 1919. Again his London centres on St Paul's Cathedral.

Town-Thoughts from Severn (p.75) GPB 2; SS 52.11.123; RMS 67.18; **DG 18.21.2**; DG 12.3.17*; BMS 64.4.8v; STU64.10.2; *PN Review 101*, 24. Also called 'Town-Thoughts from the West'. Rejected by *The Spectator* in August 1919.

On a Western City (p.76) • 2LS 19.60–61; **DG 19.59***; DG 12.3.4. The Island was a name commonly used in Gloucester for Lower Westgate, i.e. the island between 'Foreign Bridge' and Westgate Bridge. Sean Street records that at

Dymock station 'in springtime thousands of workers imported from as far away as London would arrive to help with the daffodil harvest' (*The Dymock Poets*, 1994, p.19). Gurney's experience as cinema pianist would have made him familiar with the latest films of Charlie Chaplin, Tarzan and slapstick Italians.

On a Town (p.78) **DG 21A.159***; DG 21A.160; *PN Review 102*, 27. Gurney is again praising Gloucester and England against all comparison, even Virgil's Rome and Dante's Florence. 'Realty', in some ways equivalent to 'reality', emphasises matter and the actual world; Gurney could have found the term either in legal documents where it means 'real property or estate' or, more probably, in Gerard Manley Hopkins, who calls Duns Scotus 'Of realty the rarest-veined unraveller' in 'Duns Scotus's Oxford'. 'Gloire' is French for 'fame'. Avalon is the Celtic Isle of the Blessed to which Arthur is borne after his death, while Sarras is the country to which Joseph of Arimathea fled in the Grail legend.

Blessings (p.79) • RMS 67.3v; **DG 19.125**; STU 64.10.4–4v. The poem is called 'From Robinswood Hill' in STU 64.10.4–4v and there is a Marion Scott transcript of an earlier version dated 'Gloucester. December 1918' called 'Under Robinswood' (IM 42.3.50). Robinswood Hill is about two miles south of the Cathedral and the alternative title more clearly indicates that Gurney is scanning the churches of Gloucester, its surrounding hills, its Cathedral and then the larger landscape.

Above Maisemore (p.80) **DG 12.3.19**; PMS 64.1.89v; Blunden, 52; Kavanagh, 63. The subject is again Gloucester, this time seen from above Maisemore, from where the Cathedral is clearly visible. Gurney may have picked up the archaic 'statua' from Shakespeare who uses it, for example, twice in *Julius Caesar* (II. ii. 76, and III. ii. 192).

The Town (p.81) **DG 19.134***; DG 12.2.10; *PN Review 102*, 28. Gurney's corrections on the copy-text indicate difficulties with the ending. The original typed ending offered instead of the last line given in our text:

> And hills, the Empire just an honoured name
>
> No spur to grabbing lands across seas wide.

He deleted these and added:

> And air is here as water –
>
> The hill walls hold that crystal like a font.

These also he deleted and settled on the final line about cricket.

There is no John Smith Row in official Gloucester records of the early years of this century. Smith's Passage or Back Foundry Street did exist, and the Gloucester Council minutes for 1914 record demands for the landlord to carry out repairs in the area. The *Journal* is Gloucester's newspaper, founded in 1722.

Time to Come (p.83) 1EB 55.31–31v; **DG 19.126**; DG 19.127*; Hurd, 211; Kavanagh, 107; Walter, 28. St Nicholas is a church of Norman foundation in the centre of Gloucester. Gloucester was always a crucial city in any dealings with Wales, controlling the road from London and Oxford into South Wales. In 1643 the Royalists beseiged Gloucester but failed to take it, and a significant Welsh army was destroyed at that time.

Alterations (p.84) **DG 18.45.3***; DG 82.33; BMS 64.4.21; Grigson; Kavanagh, 98. Also called 'Changes'. Stack-boards are used to protect the base of feed or grain stores from passing cattle.

Change (p.85) **DG 19.121***; DG 12.3.9; *PN Review 102*, 26.

Near Redmarley (p.86) **DG 19.119***; DG 12.2.11*; *PN Review 102*, 27. Malvern Hill, which was one of the chain of beacons ready to warn of the Spanish Armada in 1588, is visible from Redmarley.

Brave Carpets (p.87) 1EB 70.35; **DG 18.5b**; DG 64.11.23*; BMS 64.4.58; *PN Review 102*, 26–7. Syenite is a grey crystalline rock like granite. Gurney again uses archaisms: 'kine' as plural for 'cow' and 'conies' for 'rabbits'.

There is a Valley (p.88) • **DG 21A.165***; DG 64.11.17. The memories are of Gurney's reading of Charles Reade's historical romance, *The Cloister and the Hearth* (1861), Wordsworth's *Prelude* – which Gurney calls 'really and truly one of my favourite things' (*Letters*, 499) – and of playing Brahms, 'who is very much revered of me' (*Letters*, 119). The Severn Bore, a tidal wave, is highest at the equinoxes: see also 'Bridges' (p.110).

A Farmer's House (p.89) • **DG 21A.149***. The copy-text typing is incomplete, missing all but the first two words of line 16 and ending at 'Heaven' in line 20. Gurney completed the poem in black ink, but did not correct the unhelpful punctuation. He did not, for example close either of the inverted commas that he opened. We have offered a punctuation.

Valley Farm (p.90) **3LS 64.12.17**; BMS 64.4.17; Kavanagh, 135. There is one line of 'Midnight' at the foot of the page, which helps to identify this as the copy-text for those poems sent to Sidgwick. The Fortunate Isles (said to be the Canaries) were thought by the Greeks and Romans to be the seat of the blessed, where the souls of the virtuous went after death.

High Morning (p.91) • **DG 19.135***; DG 12.2.8.

This County (p.92) • 2LS 70.31; **DG 19.137**; DG 82.31*

Longney (p.93) • **DG 19.118***.

Ashleworth (p.94) • **DG 19.120***. The church of St Andrew and St Bartholomew at Ashleworth has a 14th-century buttressed tower.

The Patroller (p.95) GPB 2; SS 53.38; RMS 67.11; **DG 21A.167***; *PN Review 101*, 26. On Marion Scott's transcript IM 42.3.105 this is dated 'London. Jan. or Feb. 1919'.

Up on Cotswold (p.96) • **DG 82.37***; DG 82.1. Bob Major and Bob Minor are terms used in bell-ringing, where change-ringers use different methods to produce long peals of changes. Bob Major is a peal rung on eight bells and Bob Minor on six.

Supposition (p.97) RMS 67.4; **DG 12.3.7**; DG 12.3.12*, BMS 64.4.12v; *PN Review 101*, 25. Rejected by *The New Witness* in August 1919.

Iliadian (p.98) • **DG 19.117**; DG 12.3.11*. In comparing the wall of the Cotswolds to the wall of Troy, Gurney alludes to Homer's *Iliad*, which he knew best in the translation by George Chapman (*c*.1560–1634).

Personages (p.99) **DG 21A.150**; DG 2 1A.151*; Kavanagh, 91; Walter, 23. Gurney is finding Gloucester people the equivalent of characters in literature and legend. The orange seller is like Queen Deirdre, the beautiful but fateful heroine of Irish legend (and subject of plays by A.E. [G.W.Russell], Synge and Yeats); the woodcutter is a type of manly beauty like Apollo; the farmer has the strength of Zeus, the greatest of the Greek gods; and the girl who milks the Jersey cows is like Rosalind, the heroine of Shakespeare's *As You Like It*.

Generations (p.100) 1EB 70.33; **DG 19.32**; DG 82.36*; BMS 64.4.13; *PN Review 102*, 28; Walter, 29. The aged Gloucestershire Justice Shallow in Act III Scene 2 of Shakespeare's *Henry IV, Part 2* boasts that 'you had not four such swinge-bucklers in all the inns of court again' as the fellows of 'mad Shallow', who included 'Will Squele a Cotswold man'. John Gaunt dies in Act II Scene 1 of *Richard II*, having praised England in a speech which Gurney knew well, and having cursed Richard.

The Dursley School-Master (p.101) • **DG 21A.146**; DG 64.11.20*. R. P. Beckinsale says of Dursley that 'Local writers . . . have done their best to show that Shakespeare stayed here for a short while. A Thomas Shakespeare, weaver, was married at Dursley in 1678, and the name was by then well-known in the neighbourhood' (*Companion into Gloucestershire*, 1948, p.151). 'Circont', though probably meaning 'surrounded' or 'circled', is not in the *OED*, and may be a transcription error (for 'Circuit'?). Nilus, the Latin form of the river Nile, does not like the Severn supply 'elvers', the young eels; but in *Antony and Cleopatra*, where Shakespeare uses the form 'Nylus', it is associated with the asp: 'Hast thou the pretty worme of Nylus there / That killes and paines not.' Shallow is the Gloucester Justice from *Henry IV Part 2*, Hotspur the gallant fiery rival of Hal in *Henry IV, Part 1*, Perdita the young heroine of *The Winter's Tale*, and Viola the heroine of *Twelfth Night*. Presumably because of the Poor

Tom scenes, Edgar, Gloucester's son in *King Lear*, is placed among the clowns: Feste from *Twelfth Night*, Touchstone from *As You Like It*, Bottom from *A Midsummer Night's Dream*, and Launcelot Gobbo from *The Merchant of Venice*.

April 23 1922 (p.102) • **DG 21A.153***; DG 21A.154. This poem continues the argument of 'The Dursley School-Master' in seeing the characteristics of Gloucester in Shakespeare's plays, casting light and air into the stuffiest of scholars. Shakespeare's birthday and the day of his death are traditionally given as 23 April, St George's Day. Gurney sees Shakespeare outdoing the great writers of Athens, Florence and Rome: Aeschylus, Dante and Virgil. The curious word 'lairy' means both 'filthy' and 'cunning' and also hints at a place of refuge or lair. Gurney alludes to the two extremes of Shakespeare's art in the ethereal Ariel and the animalistic Bottom. In the final lines he refers to John of Gaunt's praise of England (*Richard II*, II. i. 31ff) and the death of Ophelia in *Hamlet*.

'Now are the hills born new in sparkling light' (p.104) **DG 21A.155**; *PN Review 102*, 27. This is printed as an individual poem but it could be a continuation of another poem, possibly 'April 23 1922' above.

Shakespeare's Day (p.105) • **DG 21A.147***; DG 21A.148. See 'April 23 1922' above. In *A Midsummer Night's Dream*, III.i.4, Quince tells Bottom the weaver that 'This green plot shall be our stage, this hawthorn-brake our tiring-house'; i.e. our dressing room; and the 'rude mechanicals' of that play first enter in 'Act one, Scene two'. Titania is in the same play, but Perdita is in *The Winter's Tale*. Gurney probably did declaim Shakespeare to the cows, imagining himself David Garrick (1717–79), author and actor noted for interpretation of Shakespearean roles. In a letter to Marion Scott of 19 April 1921, he writes that he 'walked over Horsepools today and Painswick, Cranham, Coopers with *King Lear* and Chapman' (*Letters*, 510).

April 23 1922 (p.106) **3LS 64.12.23**; 46.30.6 (*Letters*, 531); PMS 64.1.58. Gurney says in his letter that this 'isn't a bad Ode as those lumpy things go, I think.' He commemmorates 'Shakespeare's Day' (see above) by recalling tales about Shakespeare: Richard Davies's tale from about 1700 that 'Shakespeare used to poach deer and rabbits at Charlecote from Sir Wiliam Lucy, "who had him often whipped and sometimes imprisoned"'; Nicholas Rowe's 1709 memoir which recounted that 'the top of his performance was the Ghost in his own *Hamlet'* (see Stanley Wells, *Shakespeare, A Dramatic Life*, 1994, pp.11–12 and 26); and William Oldys's mid 18th-century account of Shakespeare in the part of Adam in *As You Like It*. He also recalls Ben Jonson's play, *The Alchemist* (1610) and perhaps Chapman's translation of the *Iliad* (1611) as much as Homer's epic.

May Day (p.107) • **3LS 64.12.24–25**. In seeing the May countryside as a setting for Shakespeare's *A Midsummer Night's Dream*, Gurney imagines 'tiring' or dressing rooms among the hedges and the characters from the play: Bottom, Puck, Peaseblossom, Snug the joiner, Starveling and Titania.

Roads (p.108) • **DG 21A.157**; DG 21A.158*. Gurney delights in the use of the archaic 'ancientry' for 'antiquity' and the rare 'decoratory' for 'decorative'.

Walking Song (p.109) **DG 21A.162**; Clark, 50; Kavanagh, 95.

Bridges (p.110) • **DG 19.136***. Gurney mentions the noise of the Severn Bore in 'There is a Valley' (see above, p.88). The bridge at Over was commissioned from Thomas Telford (1757–1834) in 1825 and built from 1826 to 1829. Soon after completion, subsidence occurred in the Eastern abutment, causing the masonry to open. Telford later blamed himself for uncharacteristically failing to put piling under an adjoining wing-wall.

The Companions (p.111) GPB 2; SS 53.38–39; RMS 67.7.7–7v; **DG 12.3.20***; BMS 64.4.6v–7; Blunden, 102; Kavanagh, 59; Walter, 13. On Marion Scott's transcript, IM 42.3.73–4, this is dated 'London. (92, Westbourne Terrace) Jan. 9 1919'. The last six lines, missing from Dorothy Gurney's typescript DG 12.3.20* but present in draft form right from the beginning in GPB 2, are supplied from manuscript RMS 67.7. Also called 'Companions of Travel'. As a night walker, Gurney was conscious of bright constellations like Orion, planets like Jupiter and Mars, and bright stars like Regulus.

Midnight (p.112) 3LS 64.12.17; **PMS 64.1 94v**; Hurd, 107; Kavanagh, 108; Walter, 40. The version of 'Midnight' that Gurney sent to Sidgwick consisted of only one line (see Introduction); we have used the only other available manuscript as copy-text.

Quiet Fireshine (p.113) **DG 12.3.8**; DG 17.53*; PMS 64.1.57; PTS 17.52; Kavanagh, 122. The title on the typescript has 'Freshness', which is an obvious misreading of Gurney's hand. See Kavanagh for the two-line addition of PTS 17.52.

Fragment (p.114) • **DG 21A.144**. The title is Gurney's. We have emended 'sweeter' to 'sweeten' in line 3 since the typist confuses Gurney's 'n' for his 'r' elsewhere. Realty is an obsolete form of 'reality' or matter, as in 'real estate'. See the note to 'On a Town' above.

I Love Chrysanthemums (p.115) GPB 2; 1LS 53.28v; RMS 67.8v–9; **DG 64.11.22***; BMS 64.4.8; STU 64.10.3v; Blunden, 101; Clark, 129; Kavanagh, 135; Walter, 85. Gurney's manuscript addition in BMS of 'To' at the beginning of line 6 is helpful. The STU version which is printed under the title 'Early Winter' is an asylum reworking.

The Garden (p.116) **DG 19.129***; DG 60.4; Hurd, 201–2; Kavanagh, 93, Walter, 29.

Common Things (p.117) **DG 18.37a**; DG 60.5*; BMS 64.4.67v–68; Clark, 86; Kavanagh, 119; Walter, 24. Also called 'The Dearness of Common Things'. Gurney is as attached to the proper word as to the things themselves: 'helves' for weapon or tool handles, 'censer', the vessel for burning incense.

Apprentices (p.118) 1EB 64.12.7; **DG 18.48a**; DG 64.11.25*; BMS 64.4.59; Kavanagh, 110; Walter, 27–8. Also called 'We Who Praise Poets'.

Doom's Tongues (p.119) • **3LS 64.12.29**; BMS 64.4.19v. Also called 'Stroke of Hours'.

Compensations (p.120) **DG 19.128***; DG 64.11.15; Kavanagh, 92.

The Crocus Ring (p.121) GPB 2; 1LS 53.44v; Howells; **RMS 67.17**; *Music and Letters*, vol. 1, no. 4 (October 1920), 284; BMS 64.4.9; Blunden, 22; Clark, 44; Kavanagh, 58. Dated 'Gloucester, March 1919' on Marion Scott's transcript 52.11.170.

Polite Request (p.122) • **DG 12.2.9**; DG 12.3.13*, BMS 64.4.13v. In line 6, 'ware' means 'aware'.

The Ship (p.123) • GPB 2; RMS 67.7v; **DG 12.3.6**; DG 19.24*; BMS 64.4.7v. Sent to *Harper's Magazine* in August 1919, but rejected.

The Square Thing (p.124) **DG 19.41**; DG 12.3.15*; BMS 64.4.16v; *PN Review 102*, 27; Walter, 27. St Mary's church at Norton Green has a distinctive medieval perpendicular tower.

Daily (p.125) 1EB 64.12.6; **DG 16.83**; DG 16.84*; GMS 64.3.24; *The London Mercury*, vol. IX, no. 51 (January 1924), 234; RVW 16.79; Clark, 62; Kavanagh, 82; Walter, 29–30. Also called 'Old Tale'.

The Cure (p.126) **DG 21A.145**; *PN Review 102*, 26. Mortune is the ancient name for Minsterworth in Gloucestershire.

Depression (p.127) **DG 17.13**; DG 12.3.10, PMS 64.1.33, PTS 42.2.7; *London Mercury*, vol. XXX, no. 178 (August 1934), 301; Clark, 125; Kavanagh, 91; Walter, 33. Sometimes called 'Drachms and Scruples'. Drachms and scruples are very small amounts, one eighth and one twenty-fourth of an ounce Apothecaries' weight respectively. PTS 42.2.7 has Gurney's correction of lines 6–7: 'To desire with heart's blood as lovers do / Or fortunes of music? – May death make even'.

Moments (p.128) **DG 12.3.5**; DG 19.35*, BMS 64.4.15; Clark, 100; Kavanagh, 134; Walter, 18.

Generations (p.129) **DG 12.3.18***; BMS 64.4.14v; Blunden, 100; Clark, 128; Kavanagh, 97; Walter, 17. Untitled on our copy-text; the title is supplied from the manuscript.

Index of Titles and First Lines

(For the purposes of this index, the definite and indefinite articles are ignored in titles; titles are printed in italic)